pastor Street , p 81.

CRISIS

Experiences

ISBN 085479 0756

The photo on the front cover is by G. D. Lawson. Gratitude expressed to him and to the Royal National Lifeboat Institution of Poole, Dorset, for permission to use it.

Printed and photoset by
Stanley L. Hunt (Printers) Ltd. Rushden Northamptonshire

CRISIS

Experiences

Erroll Hulse

I am the true vine John 15 v1

Carey Publications Ltd
5 Fairford Close
Haywards Heath Sussex

Other works by the author germane to 'Crisis experiences'

The Believers Experience, 176 pp. Carey Publications U.K. Zondervans U.S.A. The U.K. edition is almost depleted but a second edition is anticipated either by Evangelical Press or Carey Publications.

Local Church Practice, by various pastors, 190 pp. Carey Publications. The chapters 'The living church' and 'The glory of the Church' are apposite.

The Puritans and the Counselling of Troubled Souls, 'Foundations Magazine', No. 8. 1982. The centrality of the new birth with regard to experience is emphasised.

Reformation and the public worship of God, 'Reformation Today', No. 70. 1982.

Luther and the authority of Scripture. Cassette recording 67m (010CFC83). Luther's response to those who claimed authority because of their experiences is described. Available from Carey Recording Studios, 13 Lucastes Avenue, HAYWARDS HEATH, West Sussex RH16 1JE.

WHY CRISIS?

The word crisis is employed to denote an advanced state of tension in international relationships, or an acute state of emergency within a single nation. The word is also used in the arena of personal relationships. For instance a marriage can be in a state of crisis. The term is frequently used to describe an acute stage in physical illness and also to describe the decisive moment in a literary plot or novel. In this study the word is used to describe a great height or turning point in religious experience. For instance the outstanding crisis in Paul's life was experienced on the road to Damascus. For want of a better term then I will use 'crisis' to describe an emotionally, spiritually, or radically significant event in the Christian life.

COVER PICTURE

On July 15, 1975, the 1,500 ton tanker *Point Law*
went aground on Alderney. Half the crew was
rescued by a dinghy operating from the Royal
Lifeboat and the other members of the crew by
helicopter. The tanker subsequently broke up.
There is a parable here. British Evangelicalism
is floundering, being addicted to subjective
experience rather than sailing according to the
Word of God alone (Heb. 4:12). She is breaking
up on the rocky crags of new revelations instead of sailing the deep ocean of the infallible,
all-sufficient, and perfect Scriptures. It is not
unusual for pastors to have to rescue souls who
have gone aground, having been blown off
course from the safe highway of God's ocean
route which leads to the harbour of the
Celestial City. May this book be a dinghy from
the Royal Lifeboat and be a helicopter from the
Holy City to rescue many perplexed and
bewildered sailors in the increasingly rough
storms and seas of this generation.

DEDICATION

This book is dedicated especially to that countless number of Christians who suffer for their faith, and who, in spite of imprisonment, or other trials, glorify God by their faith and patience in affliction. The work is designed not only for the endangered described on the opposite page, but for the comfort of the majority of believers who, apart from their conversion, never have a crisis experience which would fall into the ten categories described in chapter 4. Like Enoch they walk with God. Spiritual walking signifies a steady life of faith. 'Enoch walked with God: and he was not; for God took him' (Gen. 5:24, KJV).

PREFACE

This book was written toward the end of 1983 and rounded off during January 1984 while the main body was being typeset. Though it took a short time to write down, it is the product of 30 years of experience in the Christian life. During that time much has been experienced and observed which must be examined in the light of Scripture.

As I see Church history the Kingdom of Christ has always been attacked primarily with reference to Scripture. It is true that in the first centuries controversy raged over the nature or person of Christ. Subsequent to that the adversary has assailed the Word. Firstly he worked to add to it such a heap of human tradition and garbage that you could scarce see it for the pile. The Reformation was successful in bringing the Church back to the principle of *Sola Scriptura* (by Scripture alone).

Following that there has been a long battle over the reliability of the Word of God. In America particularly the contest continues over the question of inerrancy. Here in Britain the subject under debate is the sufficiency of the Word. Some contend that prophecy continues and with it all the gifts described in 1 Corinthians chapter 12. They contend that apostles continue too. It is true that both the prophets and apostles that are claimed are of a lower order and of a modified kind, but nevertheless they are there and, whatever is said, they are there alongside the Word. This opens the floodgate of subjective experience from a source other than the Scriptures. Little wonder then that Scripture gradually declines and is moved from the place of supremacy. It is 'gut' that takes over. By 'gut' I mean that which comes from within man rather than that which comes down from heaven.

The question of whether or not the Charismatic supernatural and extraordinary gifts continue is a subject dealt with by Douglas Judisch (see bibliography), but here in the preface I draw attention to the connection between the two subjects. The baptism of the Spirit is supposed to be the open door to supernatural gifts. The idea that everything now must be the same as it was in the book of Acts explains why there is today this great emphasis on the baptism of the Spirit as a post conversion crisis experience and, why too, there is the desire for prophets and apostles.

CONTENTS

Romans: *all our resources are in God through union with Christ.*
1 Corinthians: *we have all been baptised into the one body by the Holy Spirit.*
2 Corinthians: *we are all filled with God Triune.*
Galatians: *fruitfulness is the only proof that we have the Holy Spirit.*
Ephesians: *all believers without exception are sealed.*
Philippians: *exalted theology is the answer to problems.*
Colossians: *all believers are complete in Christ.*
1 and 2 Thessalonians: *all believers are pointed back to their conversion.*
The Pastoral Epistles: *Paul commands hard work and even a little wine.*
Hebrews: *living by the truth of Christ is our power.*
James: *no power experience to escape affliction.*
1 and 2 Peter: *what are we to add to our faith?*
1 John: *the evidences that we have been born again.*
Conclusion: *we must build on the good work begun in us: we must avoid all forms of 'Galatianism'.*

WHAT ABOUT
A CRISIS EXPERIENCE?

If we omit the book of Acts we come face to face with the
fact that there is no such thing as a crisis experience
promised, commended, commanded or even suggested
in the New Testament. Throughout the New Testament
letters believers are referred back to their conversion,
their faith in Christ, their union with Christ, and, through
Christ their union with the Trinity. They are referred
there to their initial washing, their justification and their
having been set apart. Always their conversion is set
before them and never ever a subsequent crisis
experience.

In spite of this a whole tradition has been built up in
evangelism which teaches the importance of a post-
conversion crisis experience. Such an experience is
never actually explained. It is mystical. Something
happens which it is claimed lifts the person to a new
plane. The most common name for this is 'the baptism of
the Spirit'. According to different schools this baptism of
the Spirit or crisis experience is urged or taught to meet
the following needs:

11

1. Holiness of life.
2. Spiritual power for preaching or service.
3. Assurance of salvation.

The advocates of the crisis experience idea vary greatly. For instance some advocate seven conditions for the reception of the baptism of the Spirit, others five and some three.[1]

The idea of a crisis experience to equip the believer for holiness of life has its roots in Wesleyan perfectionist doctrine. The terms 'experience of sanctification', or 'second blessing', or 'baptism of the Spirit' are equated. Charles G. Finney was a great advocate of this teaching which was perpetuated in evangelicalism by A. J. Gordon, F. B. Meyer, A. B. Simpson, Andrew Murray and R. A. Torrey.[2]

The idea which has been promoted on a wide scale is that 'the baptism of the Spirit' experience is the only way in which believers can enter a higher spiritual realm. In order to promote this teaching reference is made to the low spiritual level of Christians. How can we possibly believe that they are complete in Christ? How can we possibly entertain the idea that they have it all because of their regeneration or new birth? The trend therefore is to minimise conversion and regeneration in order to establish the necessity of this special experience which many insist is the same thing as the sealing of the Spirit. They regard this as a felt experience and endorse their teaching with many references to Christian experience.

[1] Frederick Dale Bruner, *The Theology of the Holy Spirit*, p. 92.
[2] ibid., p. 44ff.

Furthermore the proponents of this view insist that you can be filled with the Holy Spirit and yet never have been baptised with the Spirit as a post conversion crisis experience.

The result of this teaching is that you always end with a division between those who 'have the baptism' and those who do not have 'it'. There are those who claim by this experience to have attained a higher realm of the Spirit. The trend is then to claim superiority in every respect in freedom of worship, quality of singing, praying and discerning the mind of God. Closely allied to the experience of 'the baptism' is the claim to the restoration of all the extraordinary gifts of the Holy Spirit for today. To what extent it is conscious I cannot say, but with the superiority that is asserted there is at the same time a constant disparagement of the weakness and low level of spiritual life of 'non-Charismatic' evangelicals. Of course this serves their purpose well because this disparagement leads many to think that the entrance advocated to a higher plane must indeed be correct. A further feature is the presentation of the apostolic church of Acts and the New Testament as a wonderful church filled with the Holy Spirit because they 'had' 'the baptism' whereas we do not have this now. On closer examination we discover that this romantic view of a gloriously exalted plane of spiritual living in the churches of the New Testament is not the case. The Corinthian church for instance, more than any other, boasted about spiritual gifts, yet it would be difficult to find an evangelical church today as bad as that one at Corinth in which division was rife, immorality rampant, and immaturity prevalent.

Now in tackling this subject I want to proceed as follows.

(1) Firstly it is essential to proclaim our belief in spiritual experience as such and also affirm our wholehearted and unreserved belief in what is called revival. With regard to that subject I am an admirer of Jonathan Edwards and regard his *Religious Affections* as a classic. Edwards knew revival first hand. He believed in the cessation of the Charismata. He allowed for many different experiences but never ever advocated a single post-conversion crisis experience. It is important to stress our faith in experience as such. Our Pentecostal friends constantly try to represent us as non-experimental and non-revival men. Also we are fully aware of the danger of mere academic or intellectual Calvinism.

(2) Secondly it is needful to prove that the New Testament letters never advocate a crisis experience for power, for holiness or for assurance. That requires to be demonstrated in a powerful and convincing manner.

(3) Thirdly it is necessary to explain the significance of the four occasions in Acts when the Holy Spirit did baptise groups of people and in the process remind students of Acts that that was not normative for converts. Large numbers are described in Acts who did not have the same experience as the 120 in the upper room.

(4) Fourthly it is helpful to comment on the experiences of Christians who claim that they have had the baptism of the Spirit. We will see that there are different experiences which can involve crisis.

(5) Fifthly, we observe that the work of the Holy Spirit in the Old Testament was tremendous. What then is the difference between the Old Testament and the New

Testament? What bearing has that on experience? How are we to understand the transition from the Old to the New?

6) Finally what is the practical application of the historic event of Pentecost and how is that related to the filling of the Spirit and the doctrine of revival? We conclude with the most important subject that could possibly engage our minds as we look out on the teeming multitudes of the world today.

CHAPTER 1

THE IMPORTANCE OF EXPERIENCE

It is important to stress the place of spiritual experience
in the Christian life. Apart from spiritual experiences to
do with conversion such as devastating conviction of sin,
ecstatic joy because of forgiveness and assurance,
fervent dedication and zeal, etcetera — there are all kinds
of post conversion experiences. Believers are sometimes
overwhelmed by a sense of God's love or can experience
joy unspeakable and full of glory. Paul described being
caught up to paradise (2 Cor. 12:4). Some believers
dream dreams and others see visions.

In my book *The Believer's Experience*[1] I emphasise the
importance of experience in conversion. This varies
greatly from the spine chilling drama of the suicidal
Philippian Jailor to the sweet and quiet experience of
Lydia whose conversion is also recorded in Acts chapter
16. Conviction of sin and joy are two major areas of
experience in the feelings and emotions of conversion.
Then there is the fullness of God's love and the direct
assurance of Romans 8:16, and sealing referred to in
Ephesians 1:13 and 2 Corinthians 1:22. The develop-

[1] Carey Publications in the U.K. and Zondervans in the U.S.A.

17

ment and enjoyment of union and communion with
Father, Son and Holy Spirit involves experience. This
subject occupies 447 pages of exposition by John Owen
which can be found in his Works (vol. 2), published by
The Banner of Truth.

On the testing side there is patience and comfort in times
of trial, tribulation and affliction. And what about
desertion which is an appalling experience? The Scriptures describe desertion and we cannot confine it to the
Old Testament. Observe that we avoid the trap of making
any of these experiences the norm. Conversion and the
ongoing Christian life can be accompanied by great joys
in some, but not all. The basic elements of experience are
the same in all believers but the expression of them is
widely diversant just as temperament and personalities
widely differ.

Experience is an essential and integral part of our
Christian faith and if we need to increase the emphasis
on this realm it is important to rely on the prescribed
means to do so. Because of a thirst for excitement many
are inclined to look for sensational things and then
regard preaching, prayer meetings, the Lord's Table and
worship services as ordinary, that is, unexciting! But the
means of grace are God's best provision, and there is no
better. Preaching will always be his best means of grace
to the end of the age (1 Cor. 1:21, Matt. 28:18-20). The
solution therefore lies not in seeking experiences for
their own sake but improving the ministry calculated to
heighten the experimental aspects of joy, power,
assurance and so on.

When it comes to the realm of experience the scope for
giving testimonies and telling stories is endless, but this

can all too soon become too time consuming and unprofitable. Many who cannot prove their case from Scripture will resort to personal anecdotes and stories. If we are going to reflect on spiritual experience it is more profitable to recall and remember times of revival although even here it is possible merely to get depressed by it. For instance there are those in Northern Ireland today who can remember a mighty movement of the Holy Spirit in 1920-1921 through the preaching ministry of Willy Nicholson. He was a rough diamond hell-fire preacher through whom hundreds were converted. Rough men from the dockland areas surged into the meetings and God met with them. After that time Nicholson went to America. He returned in 1930 and it was hoped that there would be a repetition of what happened in 1920-1921, but nothing happened. The words and expressions and methods were all the same but the power was gone. There are times of extraordinary awakening and extraordinary power but they are just that, namely extra and unusual. We should rejoice that there are such times and pray for their return. Indeed we never cease praying earnestly and urgently for our own loved ones to be converted. If we do not see great times of power we must not attempt to artificially create them. Our only resource is to use the means of grace which is precious and never to be regarded as mundane. Nor are we to despise non-revival times. We have more than enough good works to attend to even in times of non-revival.

Jonathan Edwards (1703-1758), *wrote a treatise with the title* The Religious Affections. *This is probably the most penetrating analysis ever produced on the subject of experience. The chapter headings which follow as a direct quote from Edwards' treatise not only reveal the salient thought of the author, but also provide a telling commentary on what constitutes genuine spiritual experience.*

Showing what are no certain signs that religious affections are truly gracious, or that they are not

1. That religious affections are very great is no sign
2. Great effects on the body are no sign
3. Fluency and fervour are no sign
4. That they are not excited by us is no sign
5. That they come with texts of Scripture is no sign
6. That there is an appearance of love is no sign
7. That religious affections are of many kinds is no sign
8. Joy following in a certain order are no sign
9. Much time and much zeal in duty are no sign
10. Much expression of praise is no sign
11. Great confidence is no certain sign
12. Moving testimonies are no sign

Showing what are distinguishing signs of truly gracious and holy affections

1. Gracious affections are from divine influence
2. Their object is the excellence of divine things
3. They are founded on the moral excellency of objects
4. They arise from divine illumination
5. They are attended with a conviction of certainty
6. They are attended with evangelical humiliation
7. They are attended with a change of nature
8. They beget and promote the temper of Jesus
9. Gracious affections soften the heart
10. They have beautiful symmetry and proportion
11. False affections rest satisfied in themselves
12. Religious affections have their fruit in Christian practice
    (i) Christian practice is the chief sign to others
    (ii) Christian practice is the chief sign to ourselves

CHAPTER 2

NO CRISIS EXPERIENCE
IS COMMANDED
IN THE NEW TESTAMENT

As has just been explained, there are a wide variety of spiritual experiences. One may have been endued with an empowerment for service and another have the Holy Spirit fall on him while preaching. Yet another may have a crisis experience in his or her life by which some besetting sin is finally conquered and mortified. Not for one moment do I deny that there are crisis experiences. One person may have come to assurance at a Salvation Army penitent form, another may have found victory to reconcile to his estranged parents or divorced wife. This may happen at an evangelical crusade or at some special meeting. Also many thousands would testify to crisis experiences at special rallies or large meetings or conventions. Some tell of unleashings or of deliverances. Some claim to speak 'in tongues', of liberations — and so we could go on ad infinitum.

What I am drawing attention to is the stark fact that no single crisis experience is promised, commended, held out, and still less commanded in the New Testament. Pentecost was promised and there is the outworking of that as explained in Acts 15:8,9. That is history. There-

21

[margin note:] Xians may experience crisis. Experiences according to the sovereignty of God —> but no where are they promised or guaranteed

[margin note:] The experiences in the Acts of the Apostles were individual isolated historical events —> and foundational doctrinal for our own experiences

after in no place in the New Testament is an experience per se referred to as *the* answer. You will search in vain. Always the believers are referred back to their conversion and their union with Christ. No secret key to a higher life is advocated. No escape from tension or affliction is advocated or prescribed.

As we saw at the beginning some advocate a special crisis experience as a solution for a higher life of holiness, others advocate the same for spiritual power or service, and yet others propose it for special assurance of salvation. Let us see what the Scriptures say.

Romans — all our resources are in God through union with Christ

THE way individuals conquer sin And have power in their lives is not by a crisis experience but by the harnessed the power given to them in the gospel. Our source of power is in our union w/ christ — not the baptism in the H.S.

Preoccupation with power is common today — political power, financial power, military power, nuclear power, and even physical or mental power. No power is so valuable as that which comes from the Holy Spirit when he convinces the world of sin, righteousness and judgment to come. His power to convict, to regenerate, and then on that basis to transform the lives of people is unequalled. Paul speaks of this power when he introduces the subject of salvation to the believers at Rome. He declares that he is 'not ashamed of the gospel, because it is the power of God for the salvation of everyone who believes' (1:16). This power is the experience of *everyone who believes.*

This letter to the Roman Christians is unique because of the systematic way in which justification by faith is explained together with the kind of life to which that justification leads. Once justified how does the believer live? Paul has already intimated that the righteous live by faith (1:17), but in chapter 6 particularly he goes into detail concerning the problem of sin.

How do we conquer sin? By a crisis experience? No! Rather we derive strength from Christ constantly. Paul refers all believers back to their baptism. This signifies that all our resources are in God himself. We are joined to God. What more do you want or need than that? How can you entertain sin if you are united to Christ in his death, burial and resurrection? Does Paul direct them back to a crisis baptism in the Spirit or tongues experience? No! Rather with thankfulness he directs them back to the form of teaching which they received. 'But thanks be to God that, though you used to be slaves to sin, you whole-heartedly obeyed the form of teaching to which you were entrusted' (6:17). It is not a post conversion experience he directs us to but the Gospel as a manual of teaching. This is what our Lord asserted when he quoted Deuteronomy 8:3, 'It is written, "man does not live on bread alone, but on every word that comes from the mouth of God" ' (Matt. 4:4).

Having explained that the Christian life is lived accord-ing to our resources through constant union with Christ, the apostle explains the role of the law in chapter 7 and then describes the life lived in the Holy Spirit (8:1-17). With John chapters 14-16 this forms a major definitive section on the Holy Spirit and his work in the New Testament. In these passages there is not a word to suggest that a Christian will be in a subnormal state until he has a special experience. On the contrary the Holy Spirit in the entirety of his person and work is promised

to every believer to teach, to comfort, to guide, to indwell,
to empower them for service, to help them to pray and to
assure them of their sonship, that is, of their status as sons
and daughters of God. Not one of these experiences or
activities is made contingent upon a crisis experience.
This is the very opposite of those who preach that
spiritual 'cripplehood' and 'handicapitis' (if I may coin
my own words), is the lot of all those who do not go
through what they prescribe as a baptism of the Spirit.

*1 Corinthians — we have all been baptised into the body
by the Holy Spirit*

Paul celebrates God's wisdom as that which has out-
stripped all human wisdom. The translation of 1
Corinthians 1:30 is particularly helpful in the N.I.V. It is
the mighty initiation of believers in Christ that the
apostle glories in. He declares that Christ is our
righteousness, holiness and redemption. The wisdom
that has provided such a complete salvation outstrips
every form of worldly wisdom. Not one worldly system
of philosophy has ever begun to conceive of something
of the completeness and perfection of this provision.
Thus Paul directs the attention of the Corinthians to the
complete provision that is theirs. If a particular spiritual
experience other than conversion was the key to the
spiritual life why does he not mention it?

Again he directs their attention to the threshold of the
Christian life and not to any post threshold crisis
experience, when he reminds them that although they
used to be the most foul sinners, they had now been
changed. Says Paul, 'You were washed, you were

sanctified (set apart), you were justified' (1 Cor. 6:11). This is said within the context of correcting the most inconsistent and sinful practices at Corinth such as lawsuits in civil courts against each other. He reminds them that their resources are in the Triune God and of the unity that every Christian has with the Trinity. We must never demean or depreciate that union. We never suggest, 'Oh so you only have Christ — is that all? Oh, so you are only converted — is that all? Do you mean to say that the new birth is all you've got?!'

Terrible problems of division, immorality and confusion such as drunkenness prior to the communion table afflicted the Corinthian Church, yet Paul never ever refers to a special baptism of the Spirit as an experience which raised them to a higher realm. He refers only to their baptism into Christ and their union with God. If some special power experience was the basis of Christian living, why is no reference whatever made to it in these letters, or in any of the New Testament letters?

The Baptism of the Holy Spirit of all believers without exception is described in 1 Corinthians 12:13. 'For we were all baptised by one Spirit into one body — whether Jews or Greeks, slave or free — and we were all given the one Spirit to drink.' Two verbs, you have been baptised and you have been made to drink,[1] refer to the momen-

---

[1] *ebaptisthemen* and *epotisthemen* — You have been baptised and you have been made to drink. The use of the aorist emphasises something done in the past, not something continued in the present. It is of great importance that we continue to drink the life of God daily. But the stress here is on something that has happened once and for all. The perfect tense would have been used if the ongoing results were in view. But it is the absolute finality of our union in the Triune God that is being stressed. The verbs are in the passive reminding us that this is something that has happened to us.

tous nature of conversion. All alike are baptised into the body and all alike drink of the Holy Spirit. He enters into their innermost being to work in the deep recesses of their hearts and minds. Every Christian at Corinth was baptised in water on the basis of repentance and faith (1 Cor 1:13ff.). The basis of that baptism of the believers was that they had been united to the Trinity and had become partakers of the life of the Holy Spirit.

Observe what the Holy Spirit does to every member of Christ's body. He plunges (baptises) them into Christ's death, burial and resurrection, washing and bathing them clean. At the same time he causes them to drink the living waters of the life of God so that their lives are infused and permeated with that life. Of course this involves spiritual experience and involves all the faculties including the emotions to varying degrees. The whole object of 1 Corinthians 12:13, and the context of which it is part, is to stress unity.

The most divisive thing imaginable is to deny this teaching by dividing the body of Christ into those of whom it is alleged they have the Holy Spirit properly because they have a prescribed experience, and those who do not have 'it'.

On the basis of 1 Corinthians 12:13 the conclusion is inevitable that all Christians are united in the one body irrespective of the degree of their spiritual experience, and irrespective of the spiritual gifts they possess, and irrespective of their function in the body. There are no degrees with regard to union with Christ. Either you are one with him or you are not. The same is true of the Trinity. You cannot divide the Three. Either you are at one, that is united with the Father, Son and Holy Spirit, or you are not. The same is true of drinking of the Holy Spirit. Every Christian has been made to drink of the living waters. Every Christian is a partaker of the Holy Spirit. 'If anyone does not have the Spirit of Christ, he does not belong to Christ' (Rom. 8:9). Now it is futile to drive a wedge between those Christians who may have drunk more deeply or whose experience may appear to be richer and those who may not be able to tell of exhilarating experiences. Very often the low key believers are far more reliable than the effervescent ones.

I have listened to Pentecostal teachers who spell it out very clearly that there are two kinds of Christians, those with 'the baptism' and those without. This creates the very thing that this passage of Scripture is condemning, namely, division of the body of our Lord. There is no way to prove that all the Corinthians without exception experienced a distinct post conversion crisis experience which we may call a baptism of the Spirit. It divides the Church if you insist that there are some who are essentially different from the others because they have had an experience. And then you have to define exactly what makes up this experience, and what does not constitute it, and what falls short of it. In most cases tongues is regarded as the proof that a person has the experience. This in turn leads to a variety of inducements to bring about tongue-speaking and efforts to manipulate the senses to gain this end.

Hebrews 5:11-14 speaks of infants and the mature, the weak and the strong. There is always a gradation or sliding scale from those who are new born and know very

little to those who have great resources of spiritual
knowledge. Where could you draw a line along this
scale, for how could agreement ever be gained as to
where that line be drawn? But it is very easy to divide the
church members into two camps — those with the special
baptism experience and those without.

2 Corinthians — we are all filled with God Triune

In the first letter Paul declares that believers have
received the Holy Spirit who gives understanding (2:12),
and by whom we have the mind of Christ (2:16). We can
and must distinguish the individual personality and dis-
tinctive work of each person of the Trinity but can never
divide or sever one from another. We see this in 2 Corinthians 1:21 and 22 where the three persons are distinct
yet united in their work. 'Now it is God who makes both
us and you stand firm in Christ. He anointed us, set his
seal of ownership on us, and put his Spirit in our hearts as
a deposit, guaranteeing what is to come.' Here the
concurrent working of the three persons is very clear.
Each person is distinct in person, office and work. Yet
there is such complete unity that it is never possible to
say that a believer has Christ but does not have the Holy
Spirit. Everything the Father is, the Holy Spirit is, and
everything the Son is, the Holy Spirit is. Indeed, Paul says
as much when he declares that the Lord (Christ) is the
Spirit (2 Cor. 3:17). To be filled with the Spirit is to be
filled with Christ and to be filled with Christ is to be filled
with the Spirit. The Spirit properly describes not one but
three persons. To be filled with the Holy Spirit is to be
filled with God Triune. We must resist the notion
common today that the Holy Spirit can be isolated as a

You cannot
separate the
Trinity — to
be filled
with the Spirit
is to be
filled with
Christ

separate entity. He is distinct as a personality but he can never be separated or isolated from the Father and the Son.

Paul declares that great revelations were given to him (12:7). With much modesty he describes an experience of surpassing wonder because he was caught up to the third heaven (12:2). Not only so but he possessed the gifts that marked an apostle (12:12 and 1 Cor. 12:7-12). He spoke with other languages more than anyone else (1 Cor. 14:18). Since these were a sign to unbelievers (1 Cor. 14:22) they were real languages. Yet in all this giftedness the apostle says he prefers to boast about his weaknesses (12:5,9). He says that the office of apostleship involved not only prodigious gifts but also appalling sufferings likened to those 'at the end of the procession, like men condemned to die in the arena' (1 Cor. 4:8-13).

In referring to all these signs, whether of power to work miracles or patience to bear horrific tribulation, there is no reference to a master key or a crisis experience. It is reported that Paul was filled with the Holy Spirit (Acts 9:17), but later he makes no reference to a special baptism of the Holy Spirit but rather reports his water baptism (Acts 22:16). Finally, he concludes this letter by urging self-examination with regard to their faith and Christ being in them (13:5). If it was just a matter of speaking in tongues as proof of the indwelling Holy Spirit of Christ why does he not refer to that?

Galatians — fruitfulness is the only proof that we have the Holy Spirit

The first two chapters of this letter are largely devoted to proving Paul's apostleship. This is achieved by demon-

strating that the other apostles acknowledged him as an
apostle. This shows that the apostolate was unique.
Having established his authority Paul then defends the
doctrine of justification by faith and reminds his readers
that the Holy Spirit is received by faith, that is, through
believing the Gospel. If the normal way of receiving the
Holy Spirit was by the laying on of hands or by speaking
in tongues or by breaking out into prophecies, the text
would read, 'You didn't receive the Spirit by keeping the
law did you? No! You received the Spirit through the laying on of hands and when you spoke in tongues.' The
apostle does not say that but rather plainly asserts that it
is by faith that we receive the Holy Spirit (Gal. 3:14).

Further on we come to what ultimately is the only sure
way of knowing that a person has the Holy Spirit in
salvation, and that is by the fruit of the Spirit (Gal. 5:22). If
Judas Iscariot was able to do miracles (and there is no
reason to suppose that he was different in gifts from the
other apostles) then we can be sure of this: we cannot
rely on any gift or experience. 'Many,' said our Lord, 'will
say to me on that day, "Lord, Lord, did we not prophesy in
your name, and in your name drive out demons and
perform many miracles?" Then I will tell them plainly, "I
never knew you. Away from me, you evil doers!" ' (Matt.
7:22). The above statement follows the insistence of
Jesus on fruitfulness. A good tree bears good fruit. The
fruit of the Spirit is love, joy, peace, patience, kindness,
goodness, faithfulness, gentleness and self-control (Gal.
5:22). It is no good a fruit tree saying, 'well, I've had
marvellous experiences and enjoyed refreshing rains
and I look beautiful'. The necessity is fruit. The only
evidence we have of genuine Holy Spirit indwelling is
Holy Spirit fruit.

Ephesians — all believers without exception are sealed

What are the spiritual blessings bestowed by the Father upon all those who are in Christ? Answer: election, predestination, adoption, final redemption (1:3-7). These blessings come through hearing and by faith. Referring to initial faith Paul says, 'Having believed, you were marked in him with a seal, the promised Holy Spirit, who is a deposit guaranteeing our inheritance until the redemption of those who are God's possession' (1:13).

The deposit is like the down payment which operates in mortgages in which the down payments guarantee final possession. Every believer must be 'sealed for the day of redemption' (Eph. 4:30). If you are not sealed, if you do not have the Holy Spirit, then you have no part in the day of redemption.

Whether in Romans chapter 8, or Ephesians chapter 1, the blessings are coextensive. That means that you never find some believers justified but others not, some adopted but others not, some indwelt by the Spirit but others not, some sealed but others not. This co-extensiveness is the very foundation of unity for all believers. They all have unity in the Trinity and all share the blessings bestowed by the Trinity (Eph. 4:4-6).

The confusion has arisen in the laudable attempt to raise the experimental or felt reality of the Christian blessings of adoption, sealing and assurance. I say laudable because we should feel the glory of these realities more than we do. Our faith should never be a mere intellectual exercise. In stressing the experimental side of sealing, however, a trap has been fallen into. This trap

Page 32 — Crisis Experiences

is to separate those who have a higher degree of experience from those who have a lower degree. But the Scriptures will not permit this and the text of Ephesians 1:13 will not allow it. Every single believer is sealed if he is a Christian at all. It is in the act of believing that the Holy Spirit comes to reside in a repentant soul. The Holy Spirit seals that person as his own. The felt, emotional and experimental implications of that are many and vary from person to person.

It is important that readers should not think that we are playing tricks with the text. The use of an aorist participle with an aorist verb to describe something that takes place at the same time can be seen in Matthew 19:4 and Mark 1:31. I will place Ephesians 1:13 with these, and readers may spot this usage for themselves in other places.

apokritheis eipen   he answering said
egeiren kratesas   taking hold of her hand he
                           raised her
pisteusantes esphragisthete believing you were sealed.[1]

Having described the blessings of the Christians and stressed in great detail that these are shared without exception by all believers, Jews and Gentiles (2:11–3:13), the apostle appeals to them all to walk worthy of this their great calling (4:1,2). The apostles make much of calling. Pentecostal teaching minimises calling. What

[1] The aorist participle with the aorist verb could very well be translated with the use of the word 'when'. 'When you believed you were sealed' (Eph. 1:13). The aorist denotes punctiliar time. The participle denotes time in relation to the verb it qualifies. There is an emphasis on contemporaneous action.

they say is, 'so you are only converted?' It is a tragic error to be derogatory about the new birth which is God's great act of power. Paul calls regeneration a raising up of the believer from death into the heavenly realms of Christ Jesus (2:6). There is no greater transposition than that! It is those who fail to see the magnitude of the new birth as the creation of God the Father (Eph. 2:10) who are prone to think of something else to boast about or exult in.

The prayers in this letter confirm the teaching of the fulness or the completeness in Christ of all believers without exception. It is our union which must be explored for the development of all our resources. The Holy Spirit already indwelling us is the source of all wisdom, revelation and enlightenment. His work of joining us to Christ is a work of exceeding great power (1:17-23). The method by which we are strengthened in our inner lives with power is by faith (3:17), just as the armour for spiritual warfare is the armour of faith and truth (6:12-18). This letter conveys readers to the very mountain tops of the Gospel. It is redolent with the privileges and glories which belong to all the heirs of God. At the same time it is as silent as an uninhabited part of space concerning any post conversion crisis experience.

Philippians — exalted theology is the answer to problems

Bernard Levin the famous British journalist, music critic and television personality, has written a number of books one of which is on Enthusiasm. Among the enthusiasms enthused about by Levin is of course music, followed by lesser enjoyments such as well prepared food and walking in cities. I mention this merely as a reminder of the reality of enthusiasm. What are Christians enthusiastic about? What were the apostles enthusiastic about? What are you enthusiastic about?

In Philippians Paul again shows his enthusiasm for theology — a knowledge of the Triune God. He rises to one of his loftiest descriptions of Christ when dealing with the mundane pastoral problem of conceit and selfish ambition. He appeals for humility and then employs the theology of the incarnation to show what true humility is. From the highest heaven to the lowest degradation came our Lord to gain a victory for us. Now he is exalted to the highest place with greater honour than he had before (2:6-11). The wonder of who Christ is and what he has achieved should fill us with praise and gratitude.

When the writer deals with the subject of power he suggests that our strength is something constantly supplied (4:13). He thinks of power in terms of willingness to share in Christ's sufferings even through the experience of a painful death (3:10). No easy way is suggested. Rather, Paul exhorts the Philippians to work out their salvation with fear and trembling, at the same time being confident that God is working in them and will complete that good work which he has begun in them (2:12,13 and 1:6).

Colossians — all believers are complete in Christ

As in all the New Testament letters so here in Colossians no reference is made to a post conversion crisis experience. No such thing is urged. Rather the stress throughout is to, 1. The momentous nature of what has happened in conversion, 2. The union with Christ that has been established by faith once and for all, 3. The ongoing constant requirement of discipline in the Christian life without reliance on a special experience, 4. A ceaseless dependence upon teaching as the means of nourishing and sustaining the Christian life.

In greeting the Colossian believers Paul rejoices in their faith and love that spring from their hope. His prayer for them is that they be filled with 'all spiritual wisdom and understanding', that they might bear fruit in every good work, 'growing in the knowledge of God'. He refers to a decisive action of the Father who has rescued them from the dominion of darkness, which past action is now in the continuing sense the source of their 'being strengthened with all power according to his glorious might' (1:3-13). There is no reference anywhere to a point after conversion when they learned or experienced 'the secret' of how to have this power. No! Instead the apostle goes on to stress the absolute primacy of living by faith. That is the way to be established and firm (1:23). The means of this stability and growth is teaching (1:28). All the treasures and resources for growth are in Christ (2:3), to whom all believers are joined (2:6), and in whom they are complete (2:10, K.J.V.), and have been given fullness (2:10, N.I.V.).

Conversion is again referred to as the time of new birth in which the old unregenerate person was cut off once and for all (2:11). Now we are new creatures by virtue of union with Christ (2:12, 2 Cor. 5:17).

There is no reference to a further crisis experience to complete the work of new creation. Such false teaching can only be sustained at the expense of reducing the prominence given in the New Testament to conversion, new birth, justification and union with Christ.

Thus when Paul continues to address the Colossians he points them to Christ who is their heaven now and for eternity (3:1-3). On this basis if a second blessing man asks you if you have been baptised by the Spirit you can reply by saying, 'Yes! I have been baptised with a baptism which cannot be exceeded for fulness or power because I have been baptised into the Father, the Son, and the Holy Spirit.' We do not divide the Trinity and say we only get Christ, or only have the Father, and then later get the Holy Spirit. No, we were born by the Spirit who immediately took up residence. The Holy Spirit does not live in the garage of your life until room is made for him in the house. There are not two phases, first, the garage, and later residence in the house which comes with a post conversion crisis experience. If he is living in the garage of your life then I assure you that you are not converted at all. You are a lost soul.

Particularly telling is Paul's hostility to anything which can be appealed to as a source of superiority. The church at Colosse was troubled by gnostic teachers who boasted about their special knowledge of angels (2:18). Refuting all such notions Paul insists that the believers do have everything in Christ. When they received Christ Jesus they were joined to him (2:6). That threshold, conversion, beginning or union, is the only basis upon which the entire Christian life is structured (2:6,7). Yes, we do have absolutely everything in Christ (2:9,10).

The completeness of the believer in union with Christ is supported by the concept of a new creation. A Christian can never be what he was before. The unregenerate man is gone forever. The believer is now a new creation because he has been created anew by God (3:10, 2 Cor. 5:17, Eph. 2:10). Remnants of sin remain but the believer is subject to constant renewal in knowledge and increased conformity to Christ (2 Cor. 3:18, Rom. 12:1,2).

Whatever spiritual experiences may come our way, or whatever may be our present shortfall or weakness, the fact is that every believer has complete union with Christ. Whatever lack there may be it can be supplied by the head of the Church. In Colossians Paul makes sure that there is no room for supersainthood or a higher category of any kind.

1 and 2 Thessalonians — all believers are pointed back to their conversion

Copious is Paul's reference to the time when the Thessalonians received the Gospel (1 Thess. 1:4-10, 2:13). As a consequence of this faith they all looked forward to the consummation of the second coming, a truth mentioned in every chapter of the two letters. At that second coming true faith would be vindicated. In describing the conversion of the Thessalonians features are mentioned which thrill us. In exactly the same way we are filled with joy every time there are conversions in the local church. No intimation is given that these believers were subject to a two-fold work, a first and a second blessing. The descriptions embrace only the matters relating to their turning to God from idols (1 Thess. 1:9).

Consistent with the New Testament theology of salvation, Paul brings together sanctification of the Spirit
and the Father's election and calling. He exhorts the
believers to hold fast to these teachings (2 Thess. 2:13-
15). If a post conversion baptism of the Spirit is
imperative for holy living, for assurance and for power,
why is no reference made to it?

*The pastoral epistles of Timothy and Titus — Paul
commands hard work and even a little wine*

These letters are especially important because they
provide many practical instructions as to how the
churches are to be governed, how the leaders are to
conduct worship, and how they are to provide for the
flock. A reference is made to a spiritual gift possessed by
Timothy (4:14), but no hint is given about a baptism of
power which if you believe to be imperative would
surely be mentioned for leaders in the Church of such
calibre. In the second letter Timothy is exhorted to guard
the Gospel (1:14-15), preserve it (2:2), continue in it
(3:14), and preach it (4:2). Paul has much to say about
doctrine (teaching), speaking of this 15 times in these
three letters. Teaching is useless unless it is proclaimed
to the heart in power, but no mysterious secret or key to
this power is mentioned in these letters.

As in all his other correspondence Paul urges that the
foundation upon which we build is our calling (2 Tim.
1:8). The pouring out of the Spirit he associates with
salvation, the washing of new birth, creation in Christ
and justification by faith (Tit. 3:4). We are to glory in
God's sovereign grace and in his enormous kindness in
making us heirs of eternal life (Tit. 3:5-7).

As we review these pastoral letters which provide instructions for ministers to the end of time we see that hard work is commended (1 Tim. 5:18) and the necessity of rightly dividing the Word of truth (2 Tim. 2:15). Paul even remembers to advise Timothy about taking a little wine for medicinal purposes (1 Tim. 5:23), yet he says nothing about the necessity of a distinct standard empowering experience.

Hebrews — living by the truth of Christ is our power

Hebrews 10:38 is a key text pointing to the main message of this letter. It reads, 'my righteous one will live by faith. And if he shrinks back, I will not be pleased with him'. Fearsome were the pressures upon the Hebrew believers to draw back from Christ. In order to strengthen that faith the person and work of Christ is portrayed as superior to the abrogated forms to which they were tempted to return. Christ is set forth as superior to the prophets (1:1-3), to the angels (1:4 to 2:18), to Moses (3:1 to 4:13), to Aaron (4:14 to 10:18), and superior as the 'new and living way' (10:19 to 12:29).

The eleventh chapter especially extols the importance of faith unaided by anything except promises. The best faith of all is accorded to those who believed when their experience seemed only painful, being destitute, persecuted and mistreated. Although not mentioned Job is in this category. Job's faith was exemplary when he said, 'though he slay me, yet will I trust him'.

The priority of faith exercised in difficulties reminds us that Christianity is a mixture of weakness and power, chastisements and joy. Chastisement is essential for every child of God and is not joyful but painful (12:11). The Scriptures always direct sufferers to their hope rather than reliance on their feelings or experiences (2 Cor. 5:1-4, Heb. 12:2,28). Faith exercised in the hope set before us will bring joy in our feelings but that is a happy and helpful by-product and not the main issue which is our being conformed to Christ (Rom. 12:1,2).

James — no power experience to escape affliction

Our human nature does not welcome trial and so James finds it necessary to exhort his readers to rejoice in facing trials. He commands perseverance in trial (1:12). The Scriptures have much to say about afflictions. In this way our longing to be with Christ is intensified (2 Cor. 5:2), our graces are improved (Jas. 1:4, John 15:1-6), and our understanding and appreciation of the Scriptures increased. With regard to the last named is it not true that it is through the experience of many trials that we enter into an experimental understanding of the Psalms? It is through trials and afflictions that we learn humility. Job was eminent in holiness yet expressed the humility of dust and ashes consequent to his desperate tribulations (Job 42). In the very wide sphere of affliction we never read of a simple formula or experience of power which will raise us above trials or immunise us from the pains that attend them. Innumerable are our spiritual resources and comforts in trials but no single post conversion experience is advocated to raise us above the tension of daily conflicts, or guarantee our being put outside the crucible of suffering. That a few may be healed physically is certain (5:14,15), but bodily sickness is only one aspect of affliction.

1 and 2 Peter — what are we to add to our faith?

Peter's letters begin with the foundations of election, obedience to Christ and the progressive work of sanctification by the Holy Spirit. They end with an exhortation to grow in the grace and knowledge of our Lord Jesus Christ. Especially does Peter magnify that great mercy of the new birth which the Father has given us. All that constitutes our creation in Christ Jesus; calling, new birth, faith, repentance, union with Christ, adoption and sanctification, together with that perseverance toward our imperishable inheritance, fills Peter's horizons.

Not one hint exists in these letters to support a theology of crisis after conversion. The blessings of God Triune are mightily extolled (1:2-12). The Gospel is the great and only blessing which in itself embraces all blessings (1:12). There is no second blessing as such. Indeed Peter is emphatic that in Christ we have it all. 'Everything we need for life and godliness' has been given to us. All we need is contained in our knowledge of God (2 Pet. 1:3). Yes, we are to build upon the foundations of the faith that has been given to us (2 Pet. 1:1,4). What we are to add is specified: goodness, knowledge, self-control, perseverance, godliness, brotherly kindness, love (2 Pet. 1:5-7). Surely Peter would have the prophetic foresight to see that for the duration of two millennia most Christians and almost every Christian leader would be unaware of a vital second experience which translated the recipients into an upper stratosphere of power, holy living and assurance. If ever there was a place to at least mention this experience which we are told is essential, it would be here. He is actually promising productivity and urging this as the certain way to endorse our calling and election (2 Pet. 1:8-11). Is it conceivable that he could omit something of such huge importance as that experience called 'the baptism of the Spirit'? Surely he would have said, 'make every effort to add to your faith the empowering of the baptism of the Holy Spirit, and then you will be in a position to effectively add good works, knowledge, self-control, perseverance and so on'.

1 John — the evidences that we have been born again

This letter is the only one in the apostolic testimony which deals explicitly in a detailed fashion with the subject of assurance of salvation. He plainly declares this to be his purpose (5:13). Nothing concerns God's people more than this matter of certainty. How can we be sure? It is not good enough to appeal to experience only. It is not enough to say that I have the inner witness of the Spirit and that is all I need (Gal. 4:4-6, Rom. 8:15,16). John does speak of this direct witness. 'We know that he lives in us: we know it by the Spirit he gave us' (3:24 see also 4:13). He goes on, however, to insist that we must possess the marks of new birth (What are these birth marks) birth proofs or birth evidences? Obedience to the will or law of God is one. John insists on that (2:29). The reason is that gnostic teachers were claiming to have a higher spiritual life but they did not have the birth mark of holiness. They lived in moral evil. They were children of the devil (3:10). Another essential evidence of new birth is love for others who are born into God's family (3:11, especially 14 and 5:1).

Yet another mark of new birth is that one's eyes have been anointed or opened to see that Christ is divine (2:26,

[handwritten margin note: Another way of putting it is what are the marks of God's seal on us?]

27, 4:2,3 and 5:1). We see then that the direct witness of
the Holy Spirit is augmented, confirmed, supported and
strengthened by reference to the birthmarks of faith in
Christ as God, love for the spiritual family, and
obedience to the Father's commands (5:1-6). There is not
a vestige of crisis teaching — not a word to suggest that we
should look to a special post conversion experience to
boost our assurance.

Conclusion —

1. We must build on the good work begun in us

Our confidence should be the same as the apostle Paul's,
who writing to the Philippians said that he was confident
of this, 'that he who began a good work in you will carry it
on to completion until the day of Christ Jesus' (Phil. 1:6).

The good work in us begins with a new nature. The substance of the new covenant is expressed in Hebrews 8:8-
12, 'I will put my laws in their minds and write them on
their hearts.' That is the foundation upon which all the
teaching is based in the letters we have just examined.
There is only one foundation and source of all spiritual
growth and that is the Holy Spirit indwelling us from the
time of our conversion. Jonathan Edwards states this so
well that it is hard to improve on it.

> There is not one conversion of the soul to faith, and
> another conversion to love to God, and another to
> humility, and another to repentance, and still another
> to love to man; but all are produced by one and the
> same work of the Spirit, and are the result of one and
> the same conversion, or change of the heart. And this

proves that all the graces are united and linked together, as being contained in that one and the same new nature that is given us in regeneration. It is here as it is in the first generation — that of the body, in which the several faculties are communicated in one and the same generation; the senses of seeing, hearing, feeling, tasting, and smelling, and so the powers of moving, breathing etc., all being given at the same time, and all being but one human nature, and one human life, though diversified in its modes and forms.[1]

2. We must avoid all forms of 'Galatianism'

Anything which holds out to us a route or way by which we can attain to a higher or better plane appeals to deep instincts within us. Any sincere or zealous Christian longs for the best and highest. We are all therefore vulnerable when appealed to on the basis that we could do better if only we possessed the key or secret to the higher plane.

Throughout this dispensation the churches have been vexed with divisions when false teachers have exploited the device of claiming something which will produce superiority. This appeal can be strong. After all, who in his right mind is going to travel second or third class when he can ride freely and comfortably in the first class carriage?

The Gnostics with their teaching which implied that they knew (gnosis — knowledge) something better. They could offer something superior. The Gnostics were

[1] Jonathan Edwards, The Religious Affections, Banner of Truth, p. 276.

esoteric, that is they regarded themselves as specially initiated to understand truth. John warned against them (1 John 4:3). The Judaizers added to the Gospel and thereby drew upon themselves the anathema of Paul (Gal. 1:8). The Gnostics all added to the Gospel in a subtle way in the boasting of a higher experience and thereby a superior knowledge. By doing this they earned the censure of John.

I have sought to show in this survey that there is no easy road, no higher realm that can be attained by an experience called the baptism of the Spirit. In addressing the question of sin in the life of the believer Paul declares that we have all been baptised into Christ's death and raised with him to newness of life (Rom. 6:3,4) – ALL of us, not some of us! The idea that 'mere conversion' leaves us inadequately equipped for holy living is not to be found in the New Testament.

It would seem that it is because of an inadequate under-standing of the colossal nature of God's first work of grace (Eph. 2:1-10) that some teachers postulate a second work of grace. Surely it is because of a radically defective view of the new birth that there is proneness to hanker after something additional after new birth and union with Christ. The easy believism which has prevailed for so long in evangelicalism has provided a situation in which many think of conversion as an easy thing and relatively small. They are attracted therefore by the idea of a great experience which promised to convey them by one leap into a higher realm of victorious living. In contrast the Scriptures everywhere portray the new birth as a momentous act of God. So great is this regeneration that Christ describes it as an opening of the eyes, a translation from darkness to light, a changeover from Satan's power to God's kingdom, a salvation from eternal fire to the heaven of eternal bliss (Acts 26:18, Mark 9:42-48).

X The teaching which says that mere union with Christ is inadequate is the exact opposite of the teaching of the Reformation which proclaims that we are complete in Christ. This completeness is attained by faith alone. This faith is vested in the truth of Scripture alone, and this faith receives salvation by grace alone.

X The addition of a new law which says that you are only complete when you have a post-conversion experience is a new form of legalism or Galatianism. It is adding to justification by faith alone. It is not denying justification as the foundation but nevertheless is adding to it by saying that justification is really lame until there is an additional dimension of power.

X With regard to the teaching that the baptism of the Spirit must be sought in order to gain a full assurance I have shown from 1 John that the apostle does not teach that. Rather he encourages his readers to strengthen their assurance by relating their birthmarks to their possession of the Holy Spirit. His objective is to make sure we have Christ. To have Christ is to have life, and there is no life that is better than Christ's life (1 John 5:11,12, John 10:10).

CHAPTER 3

THE FOUR GREAT OCCASIONS — AT JERUSALEM, A CITY IN SAMARIA, CAESAREA, AND EPHESUS

All Pentecostals base their baptism of the Spirit on the four occasions reported as above found in Acts chapters 2, 8, 10 and 19. It is possible to have one's mind so conditioned about these four passages that it is almost impossible to view them in any other way than in the mould that the Pentecostals have put them, namely, you get converted, then you get baptised by the Spirit, and that is what makes you a normal Christian. If you are not baptised by the Spirit then you are not a normal Christian. You are subnormal. Therefore you should seek 'the baptism of the Spirit' by means of tarrying meetings or laying on of hands. Early in my own experience I entered into Pentecostal teaching and practice. I have been through all the standard experiences of Pentecostalism including tongues. In another place I will deal with the technical matter of the physical feelings that are associated with what most Pentecostals easily accept as the genuine article. Suffice it at this point to say that I still have the greatest difficulty to get out of the groove of my old ingrained approach toward these four passages. Instead of putting myself into the position of a first century Jewish believer I find myself looking at it all as a conditioned 20th century Pentecostal.

The question is, How did the Jews view these events? To them these were occasions which proved but one issue and that is the inclusion of the Gentiles. We never find an experience being advocated or taught, and still less do we find any attempt to induce an experience. Never, ever do we find the experience itself being described or gloried in afterwards. Certainly we can discover no instance in which the Holy Spirit is preached as experience. After each outpouring Christ is central and Christ is preached and the Gospel boldly proclaimed. Moreover, we cannot find a single case of a person being left out of the four extraordinary outpourings. There is no instance described of a poor lame duck who didn't get the experience. How different this is from the modern scenes where protracted efforts are made for those who have not yet had 'the blessing'. Tarrying meetings and notable provisions of all kinds are made in which to get 'the baptism' or to attain an experience which can then be equated with 'the baptism'.

Observe too that conditions are never prescribed on any of the four occasions that we will survey in detail. Leading Pentecostalists always concentrate on preparation and conditioning. The preparations can be quite elaborate. There are conditions to be met such as earnest expectation, obedience, intense desire, purification by faith, prayer, separation from sin, reparation and restitution, joyous faith, repentance, united prayers of the church, right attitude, and so on. Pearlman advocated six conditions, Skibstedt seven, Conn six, Baur five, Riggs four, and Gee three.[1]

At Pentecost the disciples were required to do nothing but tarry which simply means wait. No effort was required. On the other three occasions reported, no conditions at all are mentioned and no preparations made. Particularly in the case of the Samaritans Peter was surprised by the total unexpectedness of what happened. As at Pentecost he or anyone else present had no connections whatever with the timing or nature of the phenomenon. It was given.

I suggest that the correct way of viewing these four accounts is to see them as a genus (a class, kind or group) that are connected together as a progression of events all the way through. They have their birth in the saying of the head of the Church, 'But you will receive power when the Holy Spirit comes on you; and you will be my witnesses in Jerusalem, and in all Judea and Samaria, and to the ends of the earth' (Acts 1:8). Those are the last recorded words of our Lord on earth. He then ascended, and being exalted to the right hand of the Father he sent the Holy Spirit to fill and possess the Church. Beginning at Jerusalem, Jesus, the head of the Church, began to build and establish one new humanity.

If Acts 1:8 is the centre of the compass point, then the complete circle by way of accomplishment, is described in two main New Testament passages, Ephesians 2:11 to 4:6, and 1 Corinthians 12:13-27.

[1] Bruner, p. 92.

Ephesians 2:11 to 4:6 tells of the unity of all believers, Jews and Gentiles, how the barriers have been broken down, how the Gentiles are heirs together with Israel, and how all believers without exception are one in one Holy Spirit, having the same Lord, the same Father, the same faith (believing the same Gospel), with the same one baptism (spiritual, into the body, which is portrayed or symbolised by physical watery baptism). Into this great Oneness all believers are brought. The question of background or race is obliterated. Samaritans, Romans, Pagans and Gentiles as far away as Ephesus in Asia Minor are included.

The 1 Corinthians passage is important because the 13th verse of that chapter is the only place outside the Gospels and Acts 1:5 and 11:16 where the baptism of the Holy Spirit is explicitly mentioned (it is implied in Rom. 6:1-4 and Eph. 4:5). We learned from that verse that every single Christian is baptised by the Spirit into the body and every single one has become a partaker of the life of the Spirit. The whole object or purpose of the 1 Corinthians 12:13-27 passage is to stress unity. It declares that, irrespective of the diversity of the members the individual members may have gifts as widely different in function as the organs of the human body, yet all the members are essentially one.

When we turn to the three extraordinary 'group events' at Samaria (Acts 8), Caesarea (Acts 10) and Ephesus (Acts 19), following Pentecost, we observe that the message of inclusion is being emphasised. In the grand historic event of Pentecost power is wonderfully displayed but it is a power which produces a united

Church. From every language group believers were
united in one faith.

Most individual Scriptures have their essential *loci*
(places of reference). As we turn now to the above-
mentioned passages in Acts, we will not regard the
events as isolated incidents, but rather as a sequence of
events which have their loci in the explanations
provided by Paul in Ephesians 2:11 to 4:16 and 1
Corinthians 12:13-27.

It will be helpful to try and assemble the data in such a
way that we can visually take it in.

Event and Place	People involved	Outstanding features
1. PENTECOST The Holy Spirit came in a new way in accordance with the promise of Christ to the Church at Jerusalem on the day of Pentecost. Acts chapter 2	120 Jewish disciples including the 11 apostles who had already received the Holy Spirit (John 20:22).	1. There was the sound of a mighty rushing wind. 2. Visible tongues of fire appeared on all of those in the company. 3. They all spoke in intelligible foreign languages. 4. They were filled with praise to God. 5. They were filled with a spirit of boldness. 6. A great work of conversion followed immediately and on the same day 3,000 converts were added to the Church.
2. An outpouring of the Holy Spirit A city in Samaria Acts chapter 8	A considerable number of Samaritans embraced the Gospel. As half-Jews the Samaritans were totally unacceptable to the Jews who would tolerate no dealings with them (John 4:9). The Samaritans were baptised as believers (Acts 8:12). When the apostles Peter and John came and laid hands on these believers they received the Holy Spirit by demonstrable visible proof.	1. Philip was used in many miraculous signs and his preaching was used to bring men and women to faith in Christ. 2. They were baptised in water in the name of Christ. 3. The Holy Spirit had not come on any of them, that is fallen upon (epipeptokos) them. 4. When Peter and John laid their hands on the believers the Holy Spirit did fall upon them but we are not told what the visible effects were. It could have been like the day of Pentecost or it could have been only prophecies and tongues. It was called 'the gift of God' by Peter. Simon the Sorcerer, who had himself been baptised, could see what it was (Acts 8:14-23).

Event and Place	People involved	Outstanding features
3. An outpouring of the Holy Spirit Caesarea Cornelius a Roman centurion and his household are converted. Simultaneously the Holy Spirit fell upon them. Acts 10:23-48	Cornelius, a Gentile invited his relatives and close friends. We do not know how big his house was, but the text says that Peter went inside and found a large gathering of Gentiles (Acts 10:27 and 15:7).	1. Peter required a supernatural vision repeated three times before he was willing to go into a Gentile household (Acts 10:9-16). 2. Cornelius was visited by an angel to give him instructions about Peter and where to find him and his address at Joppa. 3. Unexpectedly and surprisingly the Holy Spirit fell (epepesen) on 'all who heard the message'. 4. The visible proof of this was that they spoke in other languages and prophesied.
4. Conversion and union with Christ ratified Ephesus A group of 12 men are baptised and afterwards receive the Holy Spirit by the laying on of hands by Paul. Acts 19:1-7	This group were disciples of John the Baptist who had not even heard about the Holy Spirit and who needed, after they heard the Gospel, to be immersed a second time, this time not by John's baptism but Christian baptism.	1. Speaking in other languages and prophesying was the sign given that these men had indeed received the Holy Spirit.

Readers are urged to check the facts recorded above. I
have not sought to hide, restrict, omit or twist any
information. I am not in the least embarrassed by the
supernaturalism involved and have drawn attention to
each miraculous feature.

Observing the details recorded it is important to
distinguish between what is normative and what is
extraordinary. Later at a prayer meeting the building was
shaken where the disciples were assembled. It was a
shaking which assured everyone that God was with
them. Anybody who believes the Bible knows that the
time is soon coming when God will shake not a building
or two, but the whole universe (2 Pet. 3). While we all
truly believe in God's ability or power to shake buildings
we do not begin to establish as normative a doctrine that
we have not been filled with the Holy Spirit unless the
building has been shaken. Nor would we dream of taking
it to be normal that people must be struck to the ground
and blinded with scales over their eyes, as was the case
for three days with the apostle Paul.

As you examine the data listing the outstanding features
at Pentecost you will see that most of the features were
extraordinary and exceptional. Nobody has the right to
an arbitrary choice and say that he is going to insist on
literal tongues of fire on the heads of his converts. There
are a few ministers who do insist on a baptism of the
Spirit. But where do we draw the line? If there is no wind
and no fire is it real? The usual procedure is to insist on
tongues. If they are not forthcoming all kinds of inducements are employed to try and gain the required result.
The reason why I inserted the Greek word 'fall upon' was
to stress the sovereignty of the Holy Spirit's action. There

is not a single reference in the New Testament to suppose any kind of inducement. Some refer to the laying on of hands reported in the reports numbers 2 and 4, namely, Samaria and Ephesus. By no stretch of the imagination can that be construed as an effort to induce something or instruction or tutoring in order to get a desired result. There was no effort involved, just as at Pentecost the disciples were in a posture of sitting. They were relaxed. They were not trying to bring something about. The wind came suddenly at the will of God.

The wind, the fiery tongues, the ability to speak many different languages — all this was extraordinary. What can we then refer to as non-extraordinary? The outstanding fruit of a genuine visitation of the Holy Spirit is powerful preaching of the Word of God, conviction of sin, repentance, faith, willingness and desire of the converts to be baptised, great unity in the church, desire for doctrinal instruction, prayer meetings, celebration of the Lord's Table (Acts 2), assurance, joy and power to witness to the Gospel (1 Thess. 1:6ff.) and sometimes profound godly fear (Acts 5:11), combined with church growth (Acts 9:31). These features have occurred many times in church history. Even in the most powerful revivals known to us the leaders have not attempted to establish as normative miraculous signs, or sought to reconstruct the Jerusalem apostolate. The Irvingite movement of the last century did attempt to have apostles, but that movement ended in a state of eccentricity and doctrinal heterodoxy. It was certainly no revival. Sometimes attempts have been made to restore the idea of communal living, selling properties and having all things in common. That however is not normative for the simple reason that there are express commands in Scripture to tell us what is normal.

God's think @ pentecost and wsc early church was sovereign it has not commanded us to repeat these things

✗ Everybody is commanded to believe, to repent and to be baptised into the Church of Christ and to be responsible members of a local church (Acts 2:42, Eph. 4:1-16, Heb. 10:25, 13:17, 1 Cor. 12:12-26, Rom. 12:4-5). To these express commands we must add nothing. Extraordinary events are reported as God's sovereign acts and it is helpful if we observe the very simple principle that we are never to command what God does not command, or make normative what he does not specifically declare as normative. We must not add sacraments to the two prescribed, as have the Roman Catholics. Although having all things in common is reported in Acts 2 it is not commanded or specified as a duty. If there are some who feel that they are living so near the borders of heavenly love that they voluntarily agree together to sell their properties and goods and live communally, they are free to do so. But nobody should ever be put under pressure to do so. A group here in Sussex tried this procedure. It resulted in a scandal reported in the Press when one of the members of the group complained that he had been swindled by the others.

With regard to being specific about the extraordinary, reference can be made to Mark 16:9-20, which is not included in the most reliable early manuscripts. This statement refers to some special signs. One of these concerning immunity to snake-bite was fulfilled in the experience of Paul (Acts 28:1-6). We do not conclude by this that we can be careless about snakes.

Again, concerning the extraordinary, there are frequent references to angels and special visions in the early chapters of Acts. We do not oppose angels or visions. I believe wholeheartedly in angels and on more than one occasion attribute my survival to their ministry (Heb. 1:14). I am not against visions or premonitory dreams and have experienced such being fulfilled exactly as given. These are exceptional experiences which we do not have to encourage others to have. Again there is no command to seek them. Many pastors are justly concerned about personalities who by nature enjoy drama and sensation, and who by constitution have an appetite for dreams and visions. Too easily Christians can swap living by the discipline of Scripture for a pattern of life which is governed by feelings, emotions, experiences, excitements, musical entertainments and special leadings. Often those who can tell of outstanding deliverances or experiences refrain from doing so because they do not wish to feed unhealthy desires. Angelic appearances and premonitory visions are not normative. God uses angels under unusual circumstances and sends remarkable deliverances by them in times of war, or extraordinary crisis, or peril.

It is important to deal with this subject because some insist that Joel's prediction quoted by Peter in Acts 2:16-18 is normative for the church to the end of time, namely the promise of visions, dreams and prophecies. Pentecost is the fulfilment of Joel's prophecy together with the events in that generation which followed. The reference to 'the last days' is cited by some as though dreams, visions and prophecies will be normative throughout this final dispensation. That is to press Peter's citation of Joel into service which he himself would not approve. If we turn to the text in Joel we see that he is referring to that which is extraordinary and that

which constituted an historical event, namely, the
coming of the Spirit. He refers in the same context of
dreams and visions and the outpouring of the Spirit to the
fact that the 'sun will be turned to darkness and the moon
to blood'. The convulsion involved in the overturning of
the old order and the ushering in of the new is precisely
what the apostles got caught up with. That era
terminated eventually in the destruction of Jerusalem
and dispersion of the Jews. Our Lord also refers to these
traumatic events which are exceptional and not
normative (Mark 13:24). The removal of the old order is
what is meant by the sun being turned to darkness.

What is normative to the end of time is the promise of the
effectiveness of the Gospel, that all those who call on the
name of the Lord will be saved. The cataclysmic events
happen once. The ongoing work is that of proclaiming
the Gospel so that all who call on the name of the Lord
might find salvation in him.

Dreams and visions are exceptional and not the rule.
This can be illustrated in a number of ways. For instance
Dr. Thomas Barnardo had a dream which resulted in one
aspect of his work being strengthened. It was a very
simple dream. Dr. Barnardo was a typical evangelical
believer of the Victorian period whose conversion
followed in the wake of the 1859 Awakening. Dr.
Barnardo never made any claims about the Holy Spirit.
The extent of his work was astonishing. By the time of his
death 59,000 children had been cared for in his
orphanage work. Archibald Alexander in his book,
Thoughts on Religious Experience, has a chapter which
explains the place of dreams in the Christian life, and
how to know whether they are of God or not.

If we were to make a study of Christian leaders through
Church history we will find that there is a mystical
element in their lives. There are some unusual events,
leadings, deliverances, dreams and visions, but they are
exceptional, never normative. These leaders did not
make special claims for themselves. They did not try to
make the extraordinary the norm. Yet we sometimes find
Christians claiming that the Church has been
wretchedly deprived or cheated of extraordinary power
through the centuries. They claim that this has been due
to a lack of faith. When the Scriptures assert that the
extraordinary is given sovereignly it is hard to see
how the absence of the extraordinary is due to lack of
faith.

There is a copious amount of documentation to tell of the
Holy Spirit being poured out in spiritual awakenings or
revivals. But it is impossible to establish that the
extraordinary events which we have been considering
such as buildings shaking have become the norm. The
shaking of the building as reported in Acts 4 had nothing
whatever to do with the amount of faith exercised by
those in prayer. The thought of a building being shaken
like that had probably never been thought of before by
the disciples. It is much to the glory of God that he acts in
his own way and time. He is totally original. He never
consulted us about the details of the creation. The details
concerning future conversion work and future revivals
are known by him alone. They are not dependent upon
our faith.

We must now examine the four main baptism of the
Spirit passages in Acts, observing from the outset that
there are only these four which fit the description

baptism of the Spirit promised in the Gospels and then confirmed in Acts 1:8 and 11:16.

What is the message conveyed by the four groups of people, 1. Jerusalem, 2. Samaria, 3. Caesarea and 4. Ephesus?

1. Jerusalem

Everyone concedes that Pentecost was unique with regard to the 120 and with regard to the conversions that followed. The people involved were unique. There were the eleven apostles among the 120, and the 3,000 were mostly enthusiastic proselytes from many nations who had travelled great distances to be at Jerusalem for the feast. The signs of wind and fire were unique. The reversal of Babel and the gift of the person and work of the Holy Spirit was unmistakable. Note the difference between the extraordinary phenomena experienced by the 120, and what we might call normal conversion experienced by the 3,000.

2. Samaria

Why did Peter and John go to the city in Samaria where Philip had laboured? This was the first church in the making outside the apostolic circles and outside the context of Jewish faith. Ancient and bitter barriers existed between the two communities. This new church in Samaria would have been in a state of schism from the parent body from her inception unless prompt action be taken to break down the middle wall of partition (Eph. 2:11 to 3:6). For a church to exist outside of the apostolic authority would injure the unity of Christ's body from the beginning. It was vitally necessary that the inclusion of the Samaritan Christians be attested in a way that would decisively remove all prejudice. Notable is the fact that two apostles could witness to the Church at Jerusalem that the Holy Spirit had been given on equal terms to these 'half-breeds' called Samaritans, people who before had only accepted the five books of Moses and no more. By a visible proof of the reception of the Holy Spirit no voluble objection could be made to their inclusion. Thus in one stroke what was before a hostile faction, and what would have been an isolated and separate assembly, is made one in the body of Christ. This unity is precious. The manner in which the wall of division was dismantled is vivid. I suggest that it is this which should call for our admiration and praise. The purpose of this narrative is not to establish a doctrine in which each individual must be able to tell of a visible or audible reception of the Holy Spirit. The Samaritan testimony is a corporate one and not individualistic in the sense that each believer must be able to report repentance, faith and then, in addition, a specified crisis experience of physically receiving the Spirit.

3. Caesarea

It will help you at this point to go back to the record of the facts that I set before you. What happened at Caesarea with the household of Cornelius was vital as a proof of Gentile inclusion. We see this from the report of the great Council of Jerusalem. There is only one Church Council

[handwritten margin note:] Extraordinary work of the H.S. demonstrated that God accepted the Gentiles on Equal footing as the Jews.

[handwritten note at bottom:] NOTE: the gift that was given to the Church was the H.S. not the gift that was Extraordinary miracles. given was initially accompanied by signs to validate this.

reported in the New Testament and Acts 15 records it. The dispute concerned this very question of Gentile inclusion: should circumcision and the law of Moses be obligatory for the Gentile Christians?

The way had been meticulously and wonderfully prepared by the sovereign ruling of God because Peter was able to stand up in the Council at the critical point to prove that the Holy Spirit had been given to the Gentiles. This was the proof *par excellence* that they were accepted on an equal footing. This excluded any possibility of the Jews having the right to legislate for the Gentiles or impose Judaistic Old Testament laws upon them.

Peter's reference in giving a description of what happened is to Pentecost. He, the Holy Spirit had been given to the Gentiles 'just as he did to us'. He does not say 'just as he is given to everyone', but is very specific in referring to Pentecost. Peter had previously given a defence of his action in going into the Gentile household of Cornelius. The parallel passage is Acts 11:1-18. If you are a diligent Bible student you will compare Acts 11:1-18 with Acts 15:1-21. In both cases Peter describes the Caesarean episode of Cornelius and his household. He tells of the Holy Spirit falling upon (*epepesen*) them 'as he had come on us at the beginning' (11:15). The gift described is a person not an experience. The experience was the sign proving the gift. Peter says nothing at all in the two accounts about the details of the experience. Faith in Christ is stressed and faith is in the forefront. The gift proved that they had faith. These Gentiles were believers in the Lord Jesus Christ. Declares Peter, 'So if God gave them the same gift as he gave us, *who believed in the Lord Jesus Christ,* who was I to think that I could oppose God!' (11:17). On the basis that they were proven believers he commanded water baptism for these Gentiles at Caesarea in exactly the same way as he had commanded water baptism for all 3,000 new believers at Jerusalem on the day of Pentecost.

Now when the Jews heard Peter's description what did they say? What was their response? Did they exclaim, 'Praise God that Cornelius and his Gentile companions have a baptism of the Spirit!' No, they praised God saying, 'So then, God has even granted the Gentiles repentance unto life!' (11:16). Their objections were silenced and they rejoiced in the conversion and salvation of the Gentiles.

Likewise when we examine Acts 15:8,9 the emphasis of Peter is upon the acceptance of the Gentiles, acceptance to equality. 'He made no distinction between us and them, for he purified their hearts by faith' (15:9). What did the person of the Holy Spirit falling on Cornelius and his friends do? What was he given? The aorist tense used speaks volumes of meaning. The Holy Spirit was given to cleanse their hearts. That cleansing was a completed action. *Pistei katharisas tas kardias* literally translated means, by faith their hearts having been cleansed. There is no gradual process here. These Gentiles were united to Christ by faith thereby they were perfectly sanctified in the basic sense of sanctification as distinct from progressive sanctification. Writing to the Corinthians Paul describes them as having been set apart (sanctified), 1 Corinthians 1:2, and later describes them in the finished or completed sense as *washed, sanctified, justified* (1 Cor. 6:11). Contained in each word is a world of meaning. Each is a verb of finished or completed action denoting something done once and for all. These verbs are punctiliar which means full stop, nothing more to add, not possible to add anything more! Each verb is in the passive. This is something that happened to the believers. They had not actively done these things to themselves. These are actions to which all believers are passively subject. God breaks into our lives.

This is what had happened to Cornelius and his household. That is why Peter commanded them to be baptised. By the Holy Spirit's power they had believed. That they had received the Holy Spirit was confirmed in a sudden unexpected and dramatic fashion, as at Pentecost. Peter thought of the person of the Holy Spirit as he who had cleansed these Gentiles. Faith, the cleansing of the heart, and the gift of the Holy Spirit are essentially one act of God, they cannot be divided from each other.

Hence the first action to which these Gentiles were subject was washing. They had to be baptised. This meant the washing of their bodies in pure water (Heb. 10:22). Baptism or the plunging of the body into water was a powerful symbol of cleansing, once and for all washing away of the guilt of sin. This denoted a decisive action, a change of direction, an abandoning of wretched ways, and a marriage to new principles. If the Holy Spirit has cleansed their hearts then this ought to be portrayed in water baptism. Thus Peter's command. The washing of baptism lands the believer on new and holy ground. He is separated from the world. He is joined to Christ's body. He occupies new territory; a new world. He does this with all the finality that is expressed by these verbs of utter completeness, *washed, sanctified, cleansed.* Says

Peter to the Jerusalem Council 'He cleansed (once and for all) their hearts'. Note what Peter says next: 'We believe it is through the grace of our Lord Jesus that we are saved, *just as they are*' (itals mine) (15:11).

The information from Peter followed by that of Paul and Barnabas convinced the Jerusalem Council that the Old Testament promise to include the Gentiles was fulfilled (15:17). Miraculous signs and wonders among the Gentiles and the falling of the Spirit upon the Gentiles demonstrated without doubt that the Lord had saved them with the Jews on an equal footing. There is not a hint or suggestion anywhere that the peculiar operation of the Holy Spirit or of the miraculous signs were gloried in. All the way through it is salvation that is appreciated. This is the redounding music, the joy of their hearts, as is so clearly reflected when they praised God, saying, 'So then, God has even granted the Gentiles repentance unto life!' (11:18).

4. Ephesus

We have observed that on the previous occasions groups of people were embraced with nobody excluded. Here again we have a number, a small group. 'Groupness' is not the only similarity. All groups are characterised by diversity or difference from each other. Each group is unique in composition. The first one was bristling with apostles, the second was made up of despised half-breeds, the third had as their leader a centurion who, to the Jews, represented the 'overlordship' of magisterial Rome. This fourth group at Ephesus is totally different from the former three for they traced their only religious knowledge to John the Baptist. They seemed to be ignorant of Christ and of Christian baptism and did not know anything at all of the person of the Holy Spirit. Yet another difference is that they were exclusively males whereas in the former three cases the companies were mixed.

Aided by erroneous translation of K.J.V. this passage is the one most used by Pentecostals to support their claim for a separate post conversion crisis experience. The K.J.V. reads, 'Have you received the Holy Spirit since you believed?' (19:2). Much is made of the word 'since' but the text should read, 'Did you receive the Holy Spirit when you believed?' A coincidental aorist is employed in the same way as Ephesians 1:13 believing you were sealed: or, in believing you were sealed, Matthew 19:4 is another example: Jesus answering said. You cannot separate the answering from the saying. Here in Acts 19:2 *elabete pisteusantes* literally means, believing did you receive?

✗ This is a most sensible question with which to test any believer. A well taught Christian will reply with little hesitation. I was baptised as a believer into the Father, Son and Holy Spirit. It is by the Holy Spirit that I believed (Gal. 3:2 and 14). Furthermore I know I have the Holy Spirit because I have been regenerated by him (John 3:3 and 1 John 5:1), sealed by him (Eph. 1:13, 2 Cor. 1:22), indwelt by him, anointed or taught by him (1 John 2:27), led by him (Rom. 8:14), comforted by him (John 14:16), filled by him (Eph. 5:18) and sanctified by him (1 Pet. 1:2, 2 Thess. 2:13). For good measure we will add the fact that we do not have part of the Holy Spirit because he cannot

be divided. We are baptised into the Holy Spirit. We
have him!

This group of Ephesians needed the truth which Paul
taught them (19:4). They believed it and as on every
other recorded instance they were baptised in water on
the basis of faith. Would these proselytes from John the
Baptist who had now been baptised a second time in
water (this time into the name of the Lord Jesus) be
accepted by the Jerusalem Church? On the former
occasions Peter and John, and then Peter alone, had been
involved with non-Jews. They were from Jerusalem and
their testimony could hardly be disputed. In the event
their testimony about the Gentiles was accepted (15:8,9).
Paul and Barnabas had also testified at the Jerusalem
Council (15:12) but the actual decisive visible and
audible attestation of the gift of the Holy Spirit had not
been recorded in Paul's ministry. Here there were
Gentiles who possessed a partial knowledge. They lived
in the outer reaches of the orbit of those apostolic
endeavours. The Holy Spirit is poured out on them too.
All doubt and possible disputation is by one action
removed. The scope of Acts 1:8 — to the ends of the earth
— is fulfilled. Later Ephesus was to become the city of the
mother church for the church planting of Asia Minor.

The extraordinariness of what transpired at Ephesus is
not to be overlooked. We are not to conclude that each of
the twelve men received a permanent gift of prophecy
and other languages (19:6). It could have been the case,
but the purpose of the event is to provide a sign, the
wonder of which can only be appreciated when we come
to terms with the reality of all of these men being so
completely moved that God spoke through them in a

supernatural way. What a mighty endorsement of their inclusion! — what confirmation of union with Christ and the Holy Spirit!

The momentous character of this situation is appreciated when we think that it is not for us to confer this gift upon anyone by the laying on of hands. There is no Scriptural command and no New Testament warrant for anyone to lay on hands apart from the ordination of church officers to the ministry. The laying on of hands to receive the sign of the Holy Spirit was an apostolic prerogative. It was of such a dynamic and astounding order that Simon Magus who saw miracles done by Philip, seems to bypass that and rather sought this unique power (8:18,19). The subsequent severe sentence that came upon Simon Magus is a warning to all those who misconstrue the message and meaning of these passages and desire to exercise the supernatural power of God to exalt their own self importance. This realm of God giving himself to man is awesome. Ananias is reported to have laid hands on Paul, but his example is not to be taken as a licence for anybody to do the same for the simple reason that Ananias was specially commissioned by the Lord himself for his unique mission. Scripture now serves as our all-sufficient guide and we have no right to form our own canon of special revelation.

The experience of individual believers in the book of Acts

We have examined the four occasions when groups of people, varying in numbers from 120 at Pentecost to 12 at Ephesus, experienced the Holy Spirit falling upon them. But what about each individual case outside those four groups? Do we find that the apostles required that each individual should experience the Holy Spirit falling on him or her? Was it required that each individual believer should be baptised with a Pentecostal experience after conversion?

The first consideration is that of the 3,000 individuals converted on the day of Pentecost.

That such a large number could be negotiated through the waters of baptism in one day has mystified some students. Others have been more perplexed by the risk involved in receiving so many without first testing their lives for fruitfulness. This last question is more easily understood when we recall that these proselytes represented the cream of those absorbed in the religion of the Old Testament Scriptures. These were not people who had never heard of Moses, the Psalms and the Prophets. The Scriptures were preached to them by Peter as those well informed and well taught. The interpretation of those passages of Scriptures was melting in effect. Once the hearers at Pentecost saw that Jesus was the very one who had fulfilled the Scriptures there was no obstacle to immediate allegiance. The implications of the deity of Christ were such that if anyone believed that truly it spelled the beginning of a new world. Baptism represented the death to the old order and resurrection into the new. There was no point in delay. And if that issue of death to the old and life in the new is clear then there is no point in delaying baptism now. In our society the transition is often less clear than we would like it to be: hence delay.

What has delay to do with the baptism of the Spirit? The answer is that we look in vain for reference to the laying on of the apostles' hands either before or after the baptism of the 3,000. There is nothing to say that the 3,000 spoke in tongues. Nor is detail lacking, for the Holy Spirit has told us what he esteems important (2:42-47). If selling possessions is mentioned, and that is extra-ordinary and not mandatory in all the Church to the end of time, then we can be sure that if the Holy Spirit intended that every believer have his own private Pentecost of visible and audible proof, this would have been described. It is not described, and we may not build a doctrine out of silence.

Silence concerning any post-baptismal experience pervades the case of the Ethiopian Eunuch (Acts 8:25-39). Here was a man who would doubtless be a major influence in the future establishment of the Christian Church in Ethiopia, a land in which the Faith has arched the centuries to this very generation in which time numerical increases had been vigorous.

Baptism of the Spirit is so important to Charismatics that one of their leaders at the Wales Bible Week in 1983 declared: 'I believe that it is imperative for every believer to be filled with the Holy Spirit. You cannot enter into the heritage God has for you until you have received the Holy Spirit. You may as well lay aside anything else. Before you get into endtime theology, you must have this. You will not start overcoming either for it all begins here. It is a waste of time trying anything else until you've got this in order. You need to be baptised in the Holy Ghost, magnifying God in tongues, walking in the realm of the Holy Spirit.'[1] This speaker made it clear that he equated

---

[1] Harvestime cassette, 'Baptism in the Spirit', No. 1 end of side 2, Wales Bible Week, 1983.

'filled with the Spirit' with 'the baptism of the Spirit'. Now with this modern interpretation in mind let us go back to the Ethiopian Eunuch and ask how on earth Philip could be so negligent as to only baptise this chancellor of the exchequer and not tell him that it would be a waste of time him trying to do anything significant in holy living or understanding theology until he could, by a baptism of the Spirit, be elevated to walk in a different realm? Without this special baptism of the Spirit experience how could he possibly be a pioneer of the Gospel in his native land?

Even more startling than Philip's omission is the emphatic omission of God himself! Immediately the two came out of the water the Holy Spirit caught away Philip. Before Philip could say anything about a special knowledge of a higher spiritual realm he was whisked away. This is an event full of significance for it assures us that union with Christ is the highest and the best. There is no higher realm than that. There is no elevation or plateau in this life which is better than union with the Trinity. That is what the Eunuch thought because we read that he went on his way rejoicing. He had plenty to rejoice in. He had just been baptised in the name of the Trinity (Matt. 28:9). The ultimate, the apex, the best and the highest experience in this world and in that to come is union with Father, Son and Holy Spirit (1 Pet. 1:1-10, Eph. 1:3-14, Rev. 21:3,4).

Churches were multiplying in Judea, Galilee and Samaria (Acts 9:31) and Philip's services were needed. Whether we look at those churches or individuals such as Lydia (16:11-15) or the Jailor (16:25-34) we have no indication that there are any further imperatives beyond

faith, repentance, baptism and church membership.
Converts were won at Berea, Athens and Corinth but we
read nothing of a higher experience for the converts in
these places. The way in which the Gospel was
embraced at Thessalonica is described in considerable
detail (1 Thess. 1) but there is not so much as a hint there
about a post-conversion crisis experience. Our search
takes us back to Antioch in Syria and the church planting
work at Lystra, Derbe, Iconium and Antioch in Pisidia.
We read of confirming messages to strengthen and
establish the disciples (14:19-28 and 20:17-38). We read
of elders being appointed (14:23), but still there is no
suggestion that those who embrace the Gospel can never
progress, never enter a higher realm, never really
understand theology, until they have a special
experience or until they have glossalalia.

No where in the N.T. does Paul what us to seek this crisis experience.

Perhaps baptism in the Spirit as a special experience was
so fundamental that it is to be taken for granted; but not to
be able to find a single individual to present as a
prototype is asking a great deal. If this baptism of the
Spirit was higher than regeneration, the open sesame
into an elevated spiritual realm, it is simply impossible to
believe that Paul in all his writings would make no
mention of it. He tells of his experiences. He tells in 2
Corinthians chapter 12 of being caught up into the third
heaven, all this but not a word about the supposed key
experience which everybody is supposed to have. His
thesis on the way to live a holy life in Romans is
meticulous to the last Greek letter, yet nothing but
silence reigns concerning a super post conversion crisis
experience. He advocates union with Christ. He insists
on discipline and mortification by the help of the Holy
Spirit (Rom. 8:13). We look into every nook and cranny

but find no mention of this special experience which is supposed to achieve so much in a moment. I have already researched with you by examining the New Testament letters to show that no simple key, no higher experience, no crisis, no baptism of Spirit, is offered for holiness, for assurance or for power.

The normal approach for all the churches and for every single Christian is justification by faith alone. As soon as we add to that we are in error. As soon as we bring in a theology of *more*, or a doctrine of *plus* we set out on the wrong road. The life of faith is a life of faith from first to last (Rom. 1:16,17). My faith, my holiness, my assurance, my power, do not rest upon any visible or physical signs. The Bible alone is my sign. I am glad that the Holy Spirit lives in me in a mystical way which I cannot possibly explain to others (Rom. 8:15,16, 1 John 4:13). I trace that to my being baptised into the Triune God and not to any post-conversion crisis experience. There are believers who do not enjoy a strong direct assurance but they may nevertheless be more astute theologically than I, more holy too, more bold, better preachers and witnesses, for the simple reason that the Holy Spirit has not bound himself to any rule.[1] He is as free as the wind to work how and when and where he wills.

Augustine living nearer the time of the apostles made observations on this subject which will form a suitable conclusion to this chapter. It is interesting to see that of the many evidences that a person has the indwelling of the Holy Spirit Augustine is content to refer to one only, and that is love.

[1] For the Holy Spirit's work in Assurance see articles by David Kingdon, *Reformation Today*, Nos. 75, 76.

[Handwritten margin notes: Augustine → 'Tongues' was merely a sign of the authenticity of the N.S. and that the gospel was intended for every tongue & nation. The tragedy of Babel was to be reversed in the gospel]

In the earliest times, 'the Holy Ghost fell upon them that believed: and they spake with tongues', which they had not learned, 'as the Spirit gave them utterance'. <u>These were signs adapted to the time</u>. For there behoved to be that betokening of the Holy Spirit in all tongues, to shew that the Gospel of God was to run through all tongues over the whole earth. That thing was done for a betokening, and it passed away. In the laying on of the hands now, that persons may receive the Holy Ghost, do we look that they should speak with tongues? Or when we laid the hand on these infants, did each one of you look to see whether they would speak with tongues, and, when he saw that they did not speak with tongues, was any of you so wrong-minded as to say, These have not received the Holy Ghost; for, had they received, they would speak with tongues as was the case in those times? If then the witness of the presence of the Holy Ghost be not now given through these miracles, by what is it given, by what does one get to know that he has received the Holy Ghost? Let him question his own heart. If he love his brother, the Spirit of God dwelleth in him (cited by Judisch, p. 78).

CHAPTER 4

HOW ARE WE TO INTERPRET CRISIS EXPERIENCES?

'You can't take away my experience from me!' exclaims one who believes in the baptism of the Holy Spirit as a post-conversion crisis experience. Response: Nobody wants to take your experience from you and nobody can take away your experience because only you know what it is precisely that you have experienced. It may, or it may not, be an empowering experience, which I will explain presently.

We are prepared to take the Bible as our only guide for doctrine, for practice and for experience. On the foundation of Scripture I have demonstrated that no single definable post-conversion experience is commanded, commended, held out to or promised to Christians. Whatever experience you have it will avoid confusion if you call it by its right name. It may be an empowering experience, or a sanctifying experience, or an assuring experience. You may have two, three or more notable experiences. It would be sad if you allowed yourself to become complacent because of one emotional experience which must inevitably recede more and more into the past as year follows year.

There is however one experience, namely the experience of conversion, which the New Testament does encourage us to be very sure about. I have shown that throughout the New Testament letters we are urged, on the basis of union with the Trinity, to grow in grace and in knowledge. Regeneration, conversion, justification — that is the only experimental foundation upon which we are encouraged to build. We will now analyse crisis experiences under a number of different headings.

1. *In some instances the crisis experience is the conversion experience*

The evangelical climate has been one in which conversion has been simplified and made very easy. Multitudes have made decisions at various rallies and meetings. Many souls have been brought into the churches with a false assurance. Later a fiery preacher has arrived who has been the means of awakening people of this kind. Suddenly they have become alive. What they call the second blessing or consecration is in reality their first blessing, the great blessing of the new birth. Whatever they knew before that was so weak and pathetic as to deserve no such description as new birth.

It is fair to say that the practice of urging professions of faith by using altar calls or urging people to come forward and then pressing them to make a decision is more common in North America than it is here in the U.K.

Hallesby in his book on Conscience uses an apt illustration when he refers to the boy who wanted to help the butterfly out of its pupa. He said that it struggled hard to get loose. Only a few strands held it back, so the boy clipped these off. The butterfly was free and the boy was very happy both about the butterfly and about the little operation he had performed. But imagine his sorrow when he discovered what a well-meant but destructive labour of love he had performed. The butterfly could not fly and could not learn to fly. The exertions by which it was to have worked itself out of the pupa were necessary to enable it to fly. In our day we have many such awakened souls in our midst. By premature midwifery they have been helped past those birth-throes which are the necessary condition for giving birth to life.[1]

Of course the Holy Spirit will not be thwarted in his purpose. On a later occasion he will achieve his great work of conviction and new birth in the person he chooses to save. This time he will use instruments which will not frustrate his purpose. We should not be surprised, however, when we come across Christians who think they were converted when they made a decision and were baptised by the Holy Spirit later. The fact is they were spiritually dead before and what they call their baptism by the Spirit was their first great awakening.

Also common in America is the practice of accepting many spiritually lifeless people as Christians on the basis that they have accepted Jesus as Saviour but not as Lord. Until disposed to accept him as Lord they live disgraceful lives but are assured by false teachers that their lip service ensures salvation. Later, if they feel like it, they might receive Jesus as Lord. Such people are utterly

[1] I.V.F., 1962 edition, p. 48.

deceived and lost, as the Scriptures declare that without holiness no man will see the Lord (Heb. 12:14).

Nevertheless, it may transpire that through some means or other they do become truly awakened for the first time and repent for the first time, and for the first time come into union with the Trinity. This is the crisis experience for them. It is their conversion, their first blessing, not their second. J. C. Ryle, in the introduction to his well known book *Holiness*, made the same observation. The whole paragraph is worthwhile and we can observe Ryle's reasoning as he leads up to this conclusion:

J.C. Ryle's
excellent
description
of conversion
and growth
in grace

That there is a vast difference between one degree of grace and another — that spiritual life admits of growth, and that believers should be continually urged on every account to grow in grace — all this I fully concede. But the theory of a sudden, mysterious transition of a believer into a state of blessedness and *entire consecration*, at one mighty bound, I cannot receive. It appears to me to be a man-made invention; and I do not see a single plain text to prove it in Scripture. Gradual growth in grace, growth in knowledge, growth in faith, growth in love, growth in holiness, growth in humility, growth in spiritual-mindedness — all this I see clearly taught and urged in Scripture, and clearly exemplified in the lives of many of God's saints. But sudden, instantaneous leaps from conversion to *consecration* I fail to see in the Bible. I doubt, indeed, whether we have any warrant for saying that a man can possibly be *converted* without being consecrated to God! More consecrated he doubtless can be, and will be as his grace increases; but if he was not consecrated to God in the very day that he was converted and born again, I do not know what conversion means. Are not men in danger of undervaluing and underrating the immense blessedness of conversion? Are they not, when they urge on believers the 'higher life' as a second conversion, underrating the length, and breadth, and depth, and height, of that great first change which Scripture calls the new birth, the new creation, the spiritual resurrection? I may be mistaken. But I have sometimes thought, while reading the strong language used by many about 'consecration', in the last few years, that those who use it must have had previously a singularly low and inadequate view of 'conversion', if indeed they knew anything about conversion at all. In short, I have almost suspected that when they were *consecrated*, they were in reality *converted* for the first time![1]

2. In some instances the crisis experience is a leap forward in holy living

In many churches there is little doctrinal instruction and still less practical instruction on holy living. Little wonder then that when poorly instructed believers attend conferences or conventions where they are mightily moved and meet with God in a new way which to them is absolutely dynamic, they suddenly find power and resolution to give up bad habits, repent of sloth and lukewarmness, and thereafter surge forward in the Christian life. This leap forward or great stride in victorious living receives all kinds of names. I was early subject to such an experience and it was called total sanctification. With the Biblical knowledge I now have I would say that for the first time I realised what consecration meant. But as far as inward progressive sanctification was concerned all that happened was that

[1] *Holiness*, J. C. Ryle, a summit paperback, Baker Book House, p. xv.

I made a hop, a skip and a jump forward. This was laudable and commendable enough, but many miles had yet to be travelled. I now have higher views of what perfection is, namely to love God with the entirety of one's being and also to live in perfect conformity in this life with all God's revealed will. I now better understand why Paul said he did not manage to attain perfection (Phil. 3:12), and why, in spite of all our resources in Christ, he found it so difficult (Rom. 7:13 to 8:4).

Those who hold out the possibility of total, instant sanctification (sometimes called perfect sanctification, or perfect holiness) do so on the basis of certain texts which seem to teach that. But these texts belong to the category of what theologians call definitive sanctification.[1] Definitive means that the act of being set apart by God at conversion is definite and once and for all. The reference is to the basic meaning in the Greek of the word for sanctify, that is, set apart (1 Cor. 1:2, 6:11, Rom. 6:2). Having been set apart then the work of inward progressive sanctification follows (Rom. 8:13, Col. 3:5, 2 Cor. 3:18, 7:1, 2 Pet. 3:18, 1 Thess. 5:23). Ill conceived is the idea that by one mighty act of consecration perfect holiness can be attained. We are always to strive to be perfect, but at the same time realise that to love God with all our hearts and minds, means that we are constrained to confess that our best efforts still fall short of perfection.

3. *In some instances the crisis experience is unhappily no more than feelings and emotions*

It may seem very hard to some but the Scriptures insist on actual or evident fruitfulness as proof of spiritual

[1] For material on definitive sanctification see John Murray, *Collected Writings*, Banner of Truth, 1977, vol. 2, pp. 277ff.

reality. John the Baptist said that he wanted to see the fruit of repentance, not mere outward profession. Jesus said that it is no good calling him Lord if we do not do the things that he says. I have known people to give glowing descriptions of their emotional feelings but show no tangible improvement in the quality of their lives at home, or at work, or in the church.

Norman Street, pastor of Jarvis Street Baptist Church in Toronto, illustrates this matter of emotion or feeling very clearly when he refers to his ministry as follows:

> During the first fifteen years of my ministry I gave the altar call almost every time I preached. If my message had been a moving Gospel theme, there were certain persons I knew would come forward. If it was a searching sermon on the second coming of Christ, or a sermon on heaven or on hell — it would shake them up. They would come forward, weeping and asking for prayer. They always did. I used to ask myself if these people were lost and needing to be saved. I don't know that I was ever sure. Were they backsliders needing to be restored? Who could say? Many of them never did find a resting place. They reminded me of those sad words of Paul when he said, 'Ever learning and never able to come to a knowledge of the truth.' That is a tragic statement. Perhaps my message would be a strong exhortation to Christians with a challenge to renounce the world and repent of un-Christlike ways. Perhaps it would be a call to prayer, or more faithfulness in giving to the Lord. In any case, I knew that as soon as the invitation was given there would be one or two men and certain women who would come forward whether anyone else did or not. They would come down the aisle under great emotion, weeping their way to the altar.

At first, I myself as the pastor, was moved to tears because I saw in all of this, encouraging evidence that the Lord was blessing the preaching of the Word. After a while it dawned on me that there was something wrong. These sincere people never did what they were always promising the Lord they would do. They talked about it, prayed about it, and wept over it, but with all the weeping and the prayers there was never any noticeable or lasting change in their behaviour or way of life. After some years of this, I became disenchanted. I began to question the wisdom of the altar call or invitation system. I continued to conclude the service in this way, though not with the same intensity. The sad thing is that some of these people to whom I refer thought of themselves as being very spiritual. Part of what they saw as proof of their spirituality was that every time the invitation was given, they came down the aisle. After all no one can ever get too right with God, nor can anyone ever get too close to the Lord. They felt that they were always hungering and thirsting after righteousness. They felt that they were always seeking more of God. They felt that this was a sign of greater spirituality. They would even pray about others, and mention by name those they felt should have come forward. They were caught up in pure emotion and it wasn't doing anything for them.[1]

4. Some crisis experiences represent recovery from backsliding

There are instances described in Scripture of believers who grievously fall. The best known case in the Old Testament is that of David. The 51st Psalm expresses his

[1] *Reformation Canada*, Vol. 6, Issue 3, 1983.

penitence. That could be described as a crisis experience in David's life. In the New Testament we have the case of Peter who when he denied his Lord failed miserably. We cannot prove that he was in a period or state of back-sliding or decline. We can see that he was weak and sinful and needed to have a special recovery or restoration. Turning to another example we do not know enough detail to be dogmatic about the reasons why John Mark deserted Paul and Barnabas in Pamphylia (Acts 16:38). We do know that he recovered from that weak condition.

That backsliding leads to apostacy is clearly established by the letter to the Hebrews. Reclamation of backsliders is a reality. It can involve a great spiritual crisis. Not long ago a couple in our local church gave testimony that after a number of years of consistent Christian living they declined and for several years lived in a dreadful spiritual state. Eventually they were brought back to their former loyalty to the Gospel. Restoration of this kind, as we see from the restoration of the incestuous offender at Corinth, can be accompanied by deep repentance and sorrow which affects many people involved in the case (2 Cor. 7:11).

The root problem with regard to backsliding concerns commitment or consecration. Conversion includes these. You cannot be converted without being committed to Christ and consecrated to God. Too often teaching on repentance is inadequate or missing altogether. Satan is not slow to take advantage of this defect so that those who sincerely come to Christ in the first instance are easily misled into compromise and then serious sin. They must recover if they are true children of

God. Inevitably this involves a crisis of some kind or
other.

A Scottish minister by the name of James Philip has
expressed these issues clearly when he wrote:

> According to the Scriptures, conversion and
> consecration are simultaneous, in the sense that no
> conversion ever really takes place that does not mean,
> imply and involve, a true consecration to Christ. One
> does not give part of one's allegiance to Christ at
> conversion, then at a later stage make a complete
> surrender to him, called consecration. One does not
> enter into the kingdom at all except on terms of
> unconditional surrender. A believer may lose the keen
> edge of his consecration and fall away .from that
> attitude of total commitment which marked his
> entrance into the kingdom of God. If he does so, then a
> new consecration is necessary, and sometimes this is
> quite as clear-cut and decisive — and sudden — as a
> conversion experience, a crisis indeed, if this is the
> word to be used to describe it. But it is necessary to be
> clear about what has happened. It is not an advance to
> another stage of experience so much as a return to a
> previous one. A great deal depends on a true
> realisation of this. For obviously, if a believer does not
> fall away from his first consecration, but follows on to
> know the Lord ever more deeply, he does not require
> to renew it again (except in so far as our consecration is
> renewed day by day, and hour by hour, which is not
> the point at issue here).[1]

---

[1] James Philip, *Christian Maturity* (I.V.F., 1964), p. 56ff. cited in the I.V.F.
paperback *The Way of Holiness* by K. F. W. Prior in the chapter 'Crisis
on the Way'. Rev. Prior's book is highly commended.

5. The crisis of discovery

There are many Christians today who testify that the greatest crisis experience after conversion was the discovery of the sovereignty of God, sometimes called the doctrines of grace. I include myself in that category. In my search for reality I went through all the doctrines, feelings, emotions and experiences associated with Pentecostalism including the claim of the baptism of the Spirit. It was subsequent to that time that I entered a protracted spiritual experience connected with a discovery of the doctrine spelled out in the book of Romans.[1] If someone insisted on specifying *blessing number two* (however biblically inconsistent such an expression is) then I would say that my experience of free grace is my blessing number two. The word blessing or favour could refer to all kinds of mercies. To be shown the meaning of sovereign grace is life-transforming and a life-stabilising blessing. It ought never to be a second blessing but rather part and parcel of the first. In churches where the Biblical teaching is expository and systematic, new converts are born into these truths from the start. Where these Biblical teachings are absent it can be a major shock for believers to unlearn error afterwards and then come joyfully into the crisis of discovery, the discovery of the sovereignty of God in salvation.

The crisis of discovery need not be confined to the doctrines of grace. Believers can be overwhelmed by the wonder and power of the truth of substitutionary atonement, Christ actually dying in my place. This can in its

[1] A chapter is devoted to describing this experience in *The Believer's Experience*, U.K., Carey Publications. U.S.A., Zondervans.

timing and strength constitute a major crisis experience
in the life of a Christian. The attributes of God can come
with tremendous spiritual power to an established
Christian and thereby constitute a crisis experience.
There are instances in which restoration from a long
barren spiritual period is brought about by truth flooding
the soul with power. This occurred in the life of
Christmas Evans in an amazing way which is described
as follows:

> I was weary of a cold heart towards Christ and his
> sacrifice and the work of his Spirit; of a cold heart in
> the pulpit, in secret and in the study. For fifteen years
> previously I had felt my heart burning within as if
> going to Emmaus with Jesus. On a day ever to be
> remembered by me, as I was going from Dolgellau to
> Machynlleth, climbing up towards Cader Idris, I
> considered it to be incumbent upon me to pray,
> however hard I felt in my heart and however worldly
> the frame of my spirit was. Having begun in the name
> of Jesus, I soon felt as it were, the fetters loosening and
> the old hardness of heart softening, and, as I thought,
> mountains of frost and snow dissolving and melting
> within me. This engendered confidence in my soul in
> the promise of the Holy Ghost. I felt my whole mind
> relieved from some great bondage. Tears flowed
> copiously and I was constrained to cry out for the
> gracious visits of God, by restoring to my soul the joys
> of his salvation and to visit the churches in Anglesey
> that were under my care. I embraced in my
> supplications all the churches of the saints and nearly
> all the ministries in the principality by their names.
> This struggle lasted for three hours. It rose again and
> again, like one wave after another, or a high, flowing
> tide driven by a strong wind, till my nature became
> faint by weeping and crying. I resigned myself to

Christ, body and soul, gifts and labours, every hour of every day that remained for me and all my cares I committed to Christ. The road was mountainous and lonely and I was wholly alone and suffered no interruption in my wrestling with God.

After this Evans made a covenant with God pledging himself to renewed devotion to his service. Large numbers began to be added to the churches again through his preaching. In the two succeeding years six hundred persons were added.[1]

6. The crisis of empowerment

Men who have a great work to do are empowered for that work. In the chapter on what it is to be filled by the Spirit I explain what this involves for different people. A preacher needs to have unction in his preaching by which he speaks with clarity and spiritual persuasiveness. His whole mind and personality require to be taken over by God. In other words all the faculties of the preacher need to be filled and used by the Holy Spirit.

There are some like R. A. Torrey who have chosen to call their initial empowerment the baptism of the Spirit and very misguidedly sought to make that the norm for others, prescribing all kinds of ways and conditions to try and induce it. Many have read into the lives of great preachers their favourite notion of the baptism of the Spirit. I have known such advocates try and do this with George Whitefield. Dr. Arnold Dallimore, who is responsible for the foremost biography of Whitefield

[1] Christmas Evans' life, including this particular experience, is described by Robert Oliver in *Reformation Today*, No. 29.

published in two large volumes by the Banner of Truth, declares that no such claim can be substantiated for Whitefield. Rightly Whitefield is regarded as the most powerful preacher ever in the English language, and yet he himself strongly opposed the two-stage idea of Christian experience. Dr. Dallimore has written his view that to try and read into or impose a sealing of the Spirit into Whitefield's early experience is entirely in error! That every believer received 'the seal of the Spirit' was an essential element of Whitefield's doctrine and he never advocated Pentecostal teaching as it is known today.[1] Whitefield was constantly filled with the Holy Spirit. On no account could he have sustained his mighty ministry without that constant empowerment from God, a power which constantly had its source in Christ himself and not in some mysterious early post regeneration experience which modern exponents call 'the baptism'.

We have remembered Whitefield and reflected upon his powerful ministry, but what of the foremost preachers and leaders of the Christian church? What of Martin Luther? Far from endorsing the ideas of the Charismatics of his day Luther was ferociously opposed to them. During Luther's absence at Wartberg Castle the Charismatics took over at Wittenberg. It was Luther's preaching alone that brought sanity back to Wittenberg and saved the Reformation from a spirit of fanaticism and disintegration.

[1] A manuscript specifically relating to this subject was written for *Reformation Today* by Dr. Arnold Dallimore. The meticulous detail and length has precluded publication but photocopies will be supplied at 90 pence per copy which includes postage.

C. H. Spurgeon is regarded by Baptists as their prince of preachers yet he never ever advocated the idea that his power was dependent upon anything else except his full union with Christ. He never referred to any initial post-conversion crisis experience as the key to power. That idea was alien to him.

It would be possible to name a galaxy of mighty preachers of whom it could be said they were filled with the Holy Spirit but never knew, and still less advocated, a special enduement as a necessary key to successive empowerings. The word 'baptism' is preserved in its use for initiation and only occurs with regard to Pentecost and the inclusion of the Gentiles (Acts 11:16). The foremost apostle was 'filled' with the Spirit (Acts 9:17). This is important, as some deny that filling is adequate.

At this present time I could describe scenes in which the Holy Spirit has come upon congregations in a remarkable way resulting in lasting conversions. The preachers used not only to deny the notion that a special baptism of the Spirit explains the power they have experienced but are hostile to that teaching on the same basis as outlined in this treatise.

It is most important to stress that I am not denying for one moment the need to be 'anointed', or 'filled', or 'empowered', in order to have power and unction for every occasion when the Word is preached. That mentality is to be wholeheartedly encouraged in contrast to the mystical idea of relying on some past baptism of the Spirit experience.

7. The crisis of discipleship

There are some true Christians who, having grown up
with the protection and care of believing parents and a
strong local church, discover when life takes them away
from such a helpful environment that discipleship can
be much more exacting than they anticipated. The shock
can be quite severe, bringing about a spiritual crisis in
which the believer has to dive into the troubled ocean
and swim to survive. The difference between swimming
in an indoor heated pool and swimming in a stormy sea is
great. Greater dependence upon Christ leading to a new
dimension of the power of the Holy Spirit takes place.
Some look back to such a time as the real test of their
faith, but not the beginning of their faith.

Also in this class of experience is the exercise of the call
to ministerial or missionary service. This can literally
involve forsaking all for Christ's sake. It can include
leaving behind a lucrative career and venturing into an
ominous world of the unknown. A spiritual experience
which would defy any of the categories we are considering might come to such a person at such a time. That
experience will be looked back upon as a means of
strength and assurance to confirm the call and increase
the powers of perseverance and determination.

8. A crisis in the realm of assurance

This is a subject that has already been discussed in
connection with the Ephesians letter and the first epistle
of John. Suffice to say that occasionally there are those
who have an enormous problem with assurance. I say

occasionally because under a balanced Biblical ministry the vast majority of believers should enjoy what we commonly call the direct assurance described in Romans 8:15,16.

I have sometimes observed that those who come from an Arminian background into the doctrines of grace can struggle desperately over assurance for years. The reason for this is that they think back and remember that their coming to Christ was very much dominated by pressure from others keen for them to make a decision. How can they be sure that they are born again? Some Pentecostals would offer such people an experience. But that compounds the difficulty because all kinds of experiences can be induced or simulated. How can a person know whether an experience into which he has been pressed is of God? The only ultimate proof that one has the Holy Spirit is the fruit of the Spirit. Integral with that fruitfulness is the mysterious inward assurance of salvation enjoyed more by some than others.

Gardiner Spring writes on this subject in a sublime way in a chapter of his book *The Attraction of the Cross*.[1] One statement toward the end reads as follows:

> There is one way of obtaining the full assurance of hope, which is almost always successful: it is, by grow-ing in grace. Large and replenished measures of grace have a happy tendency in removing those doubts which distress the mind, and so often make it like the troubled sea when it cannot rest. They are naturally attended by increasing knowledge of the truth, by invigorated confidence in God, and by that heaven-

[1] Banner of Truth, 1983, p. 245.

imparted gratitude and cheerfulness which make the
yoke of Christ easy, and his burden light. 'Then shall
we know, if we follow on to know the Lord; his going
forth is prepared as the morning; and he shall come
unto us as the rain, as the latter and former rain unto
the earth.'

Also I have observed that those who come from a strong
Roman Catholic background often struggle with the
problem of assurance. Ingrained in their minds is the idea
that salvation is based upon good works. It takes time to
embrace fully that salvation from first to last is a free gift
irrespective of good works.

Whatever the difficulties encountered with regard to
assurance we must say that there are experiences in
which the matter may be solved. The Father may come at
any time and embrace a believer by revealing in his own
soul the greatness of his love. That is something we
cannot control. I have counselled souls to seek earnestly
the gift of full assurance. They have, and in due time
returned to say that they are no longer troubled by their
old doubts concerning the matter of their personal
salvation.

We need at this point to examine the subject of sealing. I
recommend my readers to refer again to chapter 2 and
the section on Ephesians as we deal now with the
metaphor of sealing.

A metaphor is a figure of speech in which words are used
in a literal manner to illustrate a matter. For instance, the
House of Parliament is dissolved which simply means
that the members adjourn, not that the building literally
ceases to exist. Thus we speak of the Holy Spirit

anointing and sealing those who believe. That does not mean that oil is poured on their heads or that a literal visible stamp is put on their foreheads (2 Cor. 1:22, Rev. 7:3).

The nature of sealing is that the image or character of God is stamped on the one sealed. This is done in regeneration. However regeneration is a reference to one work and sealing to another, although sealing is closely associated with regeneration. Regeneration is the transformation of the whole person while sealing refers to one of the specific results of that renewal or transformation.

Seals are used on documents to confirm or ratify them. Hence it is said that he who receives the testimony of Christ 'has set his seal to *this*, that God is true' (John 3:33, NASB). Men set their seals on that which they appropriate and desire to keep safe for themselves. So evidently, in this sense are the servants of God said to be sealed (Rev. 7:3), that is marked with God's mark.[1] They are sealed as God's own special people. Similar is the report in Ezekiel 9:4 where we read that those who really cared about God's cause had a seal set upon their foreheads, not literally of course, but spiritually.

Now every person who is born again has the image of God stamped upon him. In the same way it is said of Christ that he was sealed, that is he had the Father's stamp upon him (John 6:27). The stamp of God in regeneration is of a different order to be sure to that glorious image of the Father's fulness which was in

[1] I have actually used the words and followed the exposition of John Owen. *Works* vol. 2, pp. 242ff. See also vol. 4, pp. 400ff.

Christ. It is the imagery of sealing alone to which I am referring.

As every believer is sealed with God's stamp and image when he is born again (Eph. 1:13), so every true Christian is anointed. Anointed is to have one's eyes opened to see that Christ is the Son of God (1 John 2:27, 2 Cor. 1:22). Now there are experimental dimensions involved in these acts of God. If a person's eyes are opened he has before him a future of sight, of seeing the glory of God. Likewise if he has been sealed he has before him a life-time of assurance because the spiritual sealing has to do with ownership, that is, belonging to God. The glorious sense of belonging to God can sometimes be overwhelming as though we are being sealed all over again.

It is here that misunderstanding arises because some writers refer to sealing as an experience which takes place after regeneration. They are right in the experimental sense because it often happens that the full implications of having been sealed by God come later with varying degrees of power and realisation. It does help to avoid a lot of confusion and talking at cross purposes if we understand clearly that there is a seal or image which is initial, followed by the experimental dimensions which flow out of that initial sealing.

It is important to grasp carefully the distinctions made in Scripture and to stick to the terms used by Scripture. To illustrate the point John Calvin defined regeneration so broadly that it could sometimes be taken to include everything from initial quickening to a lifetime of progressive sanctification. As the Reformation developed the Puritans went into more detail and distinguished more carefully between regeneration and effectual calling as initial, and progressive sanctification as that which followed. Since the Puritan age, theologians have found it necessary to be even more precise and take regeneration to be the first act of God instilling spiritual life into dead souls, and the new birth in a wider context of the conscious manifestation of that new life in the Christian. One of the advantages of controversy is that it compels us to study the Bible more closely and to come to terms with the unique precision, clarity and unity that we find there.

I conclude then by saying that we will be helped if we remember that there is the initial sealing of the stamp of God on every regenerate person (Eph. 1:13, 4:30), but also many ramifications or dimensions which follow by way of spiritual experience in the life of the believer.

9. The discovery of the beauty of God

There has been a tendency to take the experiences which have consisted of overwhelming impressions of the greatness or glory of God and use them to prop up a two-tier system of first and second blessing Christianity. Even Dr. Martyn Lloyd-Jones in his zeal for revival and his desire to preserve a doctrine of power for preachers which is commendable, tended to put the label of baptism of the Spirit on experiences which were really wonderful discoveries of the power, beauty and glory of God. While the doctor vehemently rejected the teachings of the higher-life movement he did fall into the trap of the two-tier system either for power or for assurance. In order to vindicate that he tended to put all kinds of experiences into the category of the baptism of the Spirit. Let us look at one in particular. He cites the case of John Flavel.[1] In order to assess the experience we need to see it in full. Like Paul in 2 Corinthians chapter 12 Flavel speaks of a minister but we are sure, because of the intimacy of the details, that he is describing himself.

> I have, with good assurance, this account of a minister, 'Who being alone in a journey, and willing to make the best improvement he could of that day's solitude, set himself to a close examination of the state of his soul, and then of the life to come, and the manner of its being, and living in heaven, in the views of all those things which are now pure objects of faith and hope. After a while, he perceived his thoughts begin to fix, and come closer to these great and astonishing things than was usual; and as his mind settled upon them, his affections began to rise with answerable liveliness and vigour.

> He therefore (whilst he was yet master of his own thoughts) lifted up his heart to God in a short ejaculation that God would so order it in his providence, that he might meet with no interruption from company, or any other accident in that journey; which was granted him: For, in all that day's journey, he neither met, overtook, or was overtaken by any. Thus going on his way, his thoughts began to swell, and rise higher and higher, like the waters in Ezekiel's vision, till at last they became an overflowing flood. Such was the intention of his mind, such the ravishing tastes of heavenly joys, and such the full assurance of his interest therein, that he utterly lost a sight and sense of this world, and all the concerns thereof; and,

---

[1] John Flavel, *Works*, Vol. 3, pp. 57-58. D. Martyn Lloyd-Jones, *Romans* 8:5-17, p. 315.

for some hours, knew no more where he was, than if he had been in a deep sleep upon his bed. At last he began to perceive himself very faint, and almost choked with blood, which running in abundance from his nose, had coloured his clothes and his horse from the shoulder to the hoof. He found himself almost spent, and nature to faint under the pressure of joy unspeakable and insupportable; and at last, perceiving a spring of water in his way, he, with some difficulty, alighted to cleanse and cool his face and hands, which were drenched in blood, tears, and sweat.

By that spring he sat down and washed, earnestly desiring, if it were the pleasure of God, that it might be his parting place from this world: He said, death had the most amiable face in his eye, that ever he beheld, except the face of Jesus Christ, which made it so; and that he could not remember (though he believed he should die there) that he had one thought of his dear wife, or children, or any other earthly concernment.

But having drank of that spring, his spirits revived, the blood stanched, and he mounted his horse again; and on he went in the same frame of spirit, till he had finished a journey of near thirty miles, and came at night to his inn, where, being come, he greatly admired how he came thither, that his horse, without his direction had brought him thither, and that he fell not all that day, which passed not without several trances, of considerable continuance.

Being alighted, the innkeeper came to him, with some astonishment (being acquainted with him formerly), O Sir, said he, what is the matter with you? You look like a dead man. Friend, replied he, I was never better in my life. Shew me my chamber, cause my cloak to be cleansed, burn me a little wine, and that is all I desire of

you for the present. Accordingly it was done, and a
supper sent up, which he could not touch; but
requested of the people that they would not trouble or
disturb him for that night. All this night passed without
one wink of sleep, though he never had a sweeter
night's rest in all his life. Still, still the joy of the Lord
overflowed him, and he seemed to be an inhabitant of
the other world. The next morning being come, he was
early on horseback again, fearing the divertisement in
the inn might bereave him of his joy; for he said it was
not with him, as with a man that carries a rich treasure
about him, who suspects every *passenger* to be a *thief*:
But within a few hours he was sensible of the ebbing of
the tide, and before night, though there was a heavenly
serenity and sweet peace upon his spirit, which .
continued long with him, yet the transports of joy were
over, and the fine edge of his delight blunted. He many
years after called that day one of the days of heaven,
and professed he understood more of the light of
heaven by it, than by all the books he ever read, or
discourses he ever had entertained about it.

This was indeed, an extraordinary fore-taste of heaven
for degree, but it came in the ordinary way and method
of faith and meditation.

Care must be taken in every case to exercise our sense of
discernment. Temperament does enter into experiences
of this kind which makes them partly human and partly
divine. I recall when I was in Pentecostalism I became
absolutely determined to have an experience, so much
so that it is impossible to say how much was induced and
how much was genuine. Of course I am not comparing
that with Flavel who knew nothing of the modern
Pentecostal movement. I am referring to personal
disposition and intensity of emotion which is greater in

some than in others. For example John Bunyan was an
intense man by nature. He seemed to be driven almost to
despair by conviction of sin. While agreeing very much
with the need of conviction of sin, especially in our day,
we would be foolish to take Bunyan's experience as
normative. John Flavel is one of our favourite Puritan
writers. Even so we must allow for hyperbole or exag-
geration. It is difficult to believe that the bleeding he
suffered was of God. His own desire to retain the blessing
and his own physical intensity may explain that part of it.
Uplifting discoveries of the beauty of God in most cases
bring energy, inspiration and power. But I would not be
dogmatic about this matter. Experiences vary and
caution in the retelling of them is always wise. Flavel
says he learned more of the light of heaven by this than
by all his books together. We are glad that he did not
therefore diminish the diligence of his studies or the
volume of his writings. He shares with us his discovery of
God's majesty, but refrains from making any novel
doctrine of it. Nor does he try to place it in any special
category other than calling it a foretaste of heaven.

10 A crisis experience and special gifts of the Spirit

Sometimes believers claim a special experience of the
Holy Spirit which has enabled them to speak in tongues.
A number of books have been written on that subject.[1] In

[1] Among the authors on the subject of tongues are Robert G. Gromacki,
The modern Tongues Movement, Presbyt. and Ref. 1976. John P.
Kildahl, *The Psychology of Speaking in Tongues*, Hodder 1972. A. A.
Hoekema, *What about Tongue Speaking*, Paternoster, 1966. G. W.
Parnell, *Understanding Tongue Speaking*, Lakeland, 1972. Merrill F.
Unger, *New Testament teaching on Tongues*, Kregel, 1974. In the last
named book Merrill F. Unger comes to the following conclusions:

continued on page 100

the footnotes the conclusions of one of these authors is
x summarised. John P. Kildahl, a psychotherapist made an
in depth study of the subject and practice of tongues for
ten years and came to the conclusion that those with the
necessary psychological characteristics can *learn* to
speak in tongues. This, he says, gives rise to the question,
If it is truly a gift of the Holy Spirit why must it be
demonstrated and taught?[1] George E. Gardiner, Baptist
pastor in the United States and Bible Conference
speaker maintains that in his earlier experience as a
practising Pentecostalist he could get anyone to speak in
tongues if they surrendered their wills to him.[2]

Footnote continued from page 99

1. Tongues today stand unsupported by the testimony of the general
   stream of historical biblical Christianity.
2. Tongues today are manifested practically universally in a context
   of unsound doctrine. Prominent among plausible errors are (a) the
   error of construing the baptism of the Spirit as an experience of
   power subsequent to salvation, (b) the error of equating the
   baptism of the Spirit with the filling of the Spirit, (c) the error of
   connecting tongues as a sign or evidence with either the baptism of
   the Spirit or the filling of the Spirit, (d) the error of connecting the
   term 'receiving the Spirit' with a second experience after salvation,
   (e) the error of reducing the content and magnitude of the 'so-great'
   salvation purchased by Christ, (f) the error of confusing
   sanctification with a 'second work of grace', (g) the error of 'tarrying
   for the Holy Spirit', (h) the error of expecting a Pentecostal
   experience.
3. Tongues today are a major source of divisions and misunder-
   standings in the church.
4. Tongues today are not an incentive to holiness or true spirituality.
5. Tongues today run the risk of inviting demonic deception and
   despoiling.

---

[1] Kildahl, p. 74.
[2] This was stated by G. E. Gardiner in an address which is on cassette.

We can only deal with claims that are made. There is no proof that what is claimed is the same thing as we read in the Bible, especially when we remember that at Pentecost the languages were real. What we can say is that experiences as such do not necessarily have any connection with holiness of life. It is possible for unregenerate people like Balaam or Judas to have supernatural gifts and yet be lost. Having said this we still cannot argue with any person who makes a claim for his experience. All we can do is to observe the outcome over a period of time. A person may claim a great improvement and attribute that to his experience but others may have a different analysis. If there is merit or growth it is usually due to more devotion being given to Scripture.

Summary

We have seen that the subject of experience is as broad as is the complexity of manhood itself. We have also seen that crisis experiences can be due to all kinds of reasons. What we have considered is by no means exhaustive. Uncategorised experiences of all kinds are possible depending upon individual personalities and the circumstances they find themselves in. Archibald Alexander devotes a number of chapters in his book *Thoughts on Religious Experience* to death-bed experiences.[1] Some of these are truly remarkable. As always the rider must be added. They are not to be made the norm. They are recorded for our encouragement, just as are extraordinary providential deliverances reported in Scripture and in the annals of Church history, that we might take heart, give the glory to our Triune God, and determine to be faithful to him.

[1] Banner of Truth, 1967.

CHAPTER 5

THE WORK OF THE HOLY SPIRIT IN THE OLD TESTAMENT COMPARED WITH THE NEW

The unity of the Triune Jehovah requires some emphasis before we come to our subject. If only we maintained a balanced view of the Trinity we would be preserved from many errors. Most heresies spring from misconceptions of God as Trinity.

All the divine operations are ascribed to God absolutely as One. Hear, O Israel: the LORD our God, the LORD is one (Deut. 6:4, for unity of God see also Isa. 45:6-22). Yet in the unity of his being and works, Triunity appears. For instance we travel only as far as the second verse of the Bible to find a reference to the Spirit of God hovering over the waters. Now the Spirit is not just an influence or an extension of the Father. He is a person in his own right. The creation of the world is ascribed to the Father as his work, Acts 4:24; and to the Son as his, John 1:3; and to the Holy Spirit as his, Job 33:4. 'The Spirit of God has made me; the breath of the Almighty gives me life.' We are bound to note that the three persons are one in essence and undivided in all their operations. While

THE Trinity and Their work: Explained

there is always undivided unity of nature as God, and concurrence in all actions, there is also very clearly distinction of office. Thus we see the Father as Originator, Governor, Law-giver; the Son as servant, mediator, redeemer, intercessor; and the Holy Spirit as regenerator, sanctifier, and applier of that grace that has been predestined for us by the Father, and procured by the Son. As there is distinction of office, so also there is distinction in character. The Father cannot be seen. He dwells in a light which no man can approach, still less see and survive (1 Tim. 6:16). The Son is manifested by way of theopany and incarnation. He can be seen and will be seen (1 John 3:2). While the Son is localised he is in his essence God omniscient and omnipresent. The Holy Spirit is manifested as breath (Hebrew *Ruah*), or wind. His divine attributes of omniscience, omnipresence and omnipotence are especially prominent (Gen. 1:2, Zech. 4:6, Psa. 104:30).

THE work
of the Spirit
in the O.T.
3

Having taken note of the unity of the three persons of the Godhead we will now reflect on the magnitude of the Spirit's work in the Old Testament. The Holy Spirit created the world, preserved Noah, and created many languages at Babel. Then the Spirit wrought greater miracles on a national scale through Moses than anyone else including Christ. For drama and power who can equal Moses?

Then the Holy Spirit inspired a volume of literature much more comprehensive and varied than the New Testament. Think for instance of the breadth of the books by Isaiah, Jeremiah and Ezekiel. Remember too the wisdom books, Proverbs, Job, Psalms and Ecclesiastes. Of course the Scriptures of the Old Testament accumulated

over several centuries whereas those of the New
Testament were inspired almost within a single
generation.

When considering miracles of power we recall the lives
of Elijah and Elisha. For instance, remember Mount
Carmel and the descent of fire from heaven to devour not
only the sacrifice but the altar as well.

The Holy Spirit translated Enoch and Elijah physically
out of this world so that they did not experience death.
We do not know of anyone in our age who has been
translated like that.

We turn now from the immensity of the Spirit's work in
Old Testament times to another important factor. Have
you ever considered that the way of salvation by faith
was exactly the same for every Old Testament believer
as it is for us? Abraham and David were justified by faith
(Gal. 3:6-9, Rom. 4:1-8). The faith of Abraham is described in detail in Hebrews chapter 11. That chapter tells
us too of the faith of Abel, of Enoch and Noah. And then
there are Isaac, Jacob, Joseph and Moses. They were all
men of faith. Rahab the prostitute is commended for her
faith. It is faith that made men like Gideon, Barak,
Samson, David and Samuel to be courageous leaders.
The names of martyrs are not given but there were those
who suffered as much as the many Christian martyrs of
this dispensation. We read of some who were stoned and
of others sawn in two. The faith of all these, whether men
of ancient times, patriarchs, leaders, prophets or martyrs,
was a faith born of regeneration. Faith does not grow out
of the soil of fallen human nature. 'The man without the
Spirit does not accept the things which come from the

Spirit of God for they are foolishness to him,' is as true of the Old Testament period as it is of the New.

In the same way we recall the famous assertion of Jesus concerning the necessity of the new birth, 'unless a man is born again he cannot see the kingdom of God' (John 3:3). We can take this to mean that he cannot see by way of understanding or we can take it to mean that he will never see the kingdom of God by way of entrance into it. Both are true. Certainly it must be affirmed that no person can be admitted to heaven unless his old evil unregenerate heart has been removed and a new heart of love put there instead. The main issue is that hatred is exchanged for love. 'The sinful mind is hostile to God' (Rom. 8:7). This sinful mind which is at enmity to God was removed in all Old Testament believers and thereupon followed a work of the Spirit in their lives to make them holy and prepare them for the world to come.

John Owen, that Prince of the Puritans, states this matter well when he declares, 'Regeneration by the Holy Spirit is the *same work*, for the *kind* of it (the italics are his), and wrought by the same power of the Spirit in all that are regenerate, or ever were, or shall be so, from the beginning of the world unto the end thereof.' He goes on to state that 'the elect of God were not regenerate one way, by one kind of operation of the Holy Spirit, under the Old Testament and those under the New Testament by another', and 'the state whereinto men are brought by regeneration is the same. Nor is it, in its essence or nature, capable of degrees, so that one should be more regenerate than another. Every one that is born of God is equally so, though one may be more beautiful than another, as having the image of his heavenly Father more evidently impressed on him though not more truly.

Men may be more or less holy, more or less sanctified,
but they cannot be more or less regenerate. All children
that are born into the world are equally born, though
some quickly outstrip others — there was but one kind of
regeneration in this world, the essential form of it being
specifically the same in all.'[1]

We can move forward and say that the work of making
believers holy in life and conduct was the same for the
Old Testament believers as it is for the New. Without
holiness no man will see God, is as true for them as it is for
us. The purpose of regeneration is to begin a good work
which is completed (Phil. 1:6). God's work is never
frustrated. We discover that the whole range of spiritual
experiences and sensitivities to which we are subject are
described by the psalm writers of the Old Testament.
Hunger for God was as desperate as it is with us (Psa. 42),
repentance as deep and sincere (Psa. 51), joy as ecstatic
(Psa. 148), prayer as urgent and agonising (Psa. 44),
worship as intense (Psa. 84).

Well then, you may exclaim, what *is* the difference
between the Old Testament and New Testament? If as
you say the work of the Holy Spirit is basically the same
in regeneration and progressive sanctification in all
believers of the Old Testament times and the New
Testament times, then what difference did Pentecost
make? Why did our Lord make so much of the Promise of
the Spirit and why is that promise so clearly defined in
Galatians 3:14, 'He redeemed us in order that the
blessing given to Abraham might come to the Gentiles
through Christ Jesus, so that by faith we might receive
the promise of the Spirit'?

[1] John Owen, *Works*, Vol. 3, pp. 213-215.

In answer to these questions I would suggest that in the first place there was the establishment of an entirely new order, and in the second place there was a difference of degree in the Holy Spirit's work, a difference in, 1 Clarity, 2. Intimacy and 3. Abundance.

Firstly a new order. Pentecost is the establishment of the Church as the new covenant people of God: the body of Christ (Eph. 2:11–4:6).[1] The gift of the Spirit was the gift of Christ himself to his Church. Before he could only share his bodily presence with a few at a time. Now he is with all his people in all nations by his Spirit. But there is a difference from the Old Testament. He is with them now as the mediator of the New and better covenant. He is with them in the power of his accomplishment of salvation in all its aspects. The tongues of fire resting on each one at Pentecost (Acts 2:3), signifies the refining and purifying work of the Spirit (Mal. 3:1-3). John baptised with water but Jesus with fire and the Holy Spirit. Jesus needed no purification. The Holy Spirit descended on him in the form of a dove. We do need purification and we are cleansed by the blood of Jesus Christ shed for us (1 John 1:7-9).

As the Gospels record the accomplishment of salvation by the Messiah so the book of Acts records the coming of the Spirit. As the death, resurrection and ascension cannot be repeated so the epochal event of Pentecost cannot be rerun. As Christ was given to the world so the Holy Spirit was given to the Church first at Pentecost. You can only have one first time event. There were the

[1] Richard B. Gaffin, Jr., *Perspectives on Pentecost*, Pres. and Ref., pp. 20ff.

confirmatory events at Samaria, Caesarea and Ephesus which we have looked at in detail. We do not now need any further proof that the gift of the Holy Spirit in the entirety of his person and work is given to every one who is united to Christ by faith.

The Holy Spirit came at Pentecost to attest Christ's exaltation (Acts 2:33), to take Christ's place (John 14:16-18), to extend Christ's kingdom (Acts 1:8), and to endue Christ's servants (Luke 24:49). He came to *rest* on each one of them. He came to stay (Acts 2:3).

Secondly we consider the subject of degree. The Holy Spirit's work in the New Testament exceeds that in the Old Testament with regard to, 1. Clarity, 2. Intimacy and 3. Abundance.

As for clarity remember how slow the twelve were to understand what he was talking about when he repeatedly warned them about his impending death and resurrection. After the coming of the Spirit at Pentecost all the Old Testament Scriptures seemed to fall into place. What was not clear before was now like the light of the sun on a cloudless day. Even John the Baptist, by way of proximity to Jesus, was greater than all the Old Testament prophets. He could actually point to him and say, 'Look, the Lamb of God, who takes away the sin of the world' (John 1:29). Yet in a time of discouragement John sent a message to Jesus which revealed his doubts about him (Matt. 11:2). When it comes to clarity of understanding the most humble believer is greater than John the Baptist. With the New Testament in our hands we can understand the Old Testament better than the Old Testament authors themselves did when they wrote it.

2.2 In Itimou
3

Our second point concerns intimacy. Not only do believers of the New Testament enjoy a much clearer understanding of God, they also advance with regard to the subject of intimate union and communion with the Trinity. This is especially outlined for us in Romans chapter 8. Through Christ Jesus our minds are now controlled by the Spirit. He is called the Spirit of adoption because of the assurance and joy he engenders within us as God's sons and daughters. Adoption represents the apex of our privilege as God's love is shed abroad in our hearts (Rom. 8:15,16, Gal. 4:6).

There is progression in the experience of our adoption and enjoyment of the Father's complacent love (John 14:23) — a progression from the Old Testament to the New Testament and then further a progression in the next world. The progression from this epoch to that of the future world is highlighted by the resurrection as described in 1 Corinthians chapter 15. In verse 20 Christ's resurrection is called the first fruits. The Father will accomplish for all believers what he has done for Christ, namely, glorify their bodies in a bodily resurrection. They will then be equipped as citizens of the New Jerusalem.

There they will see Christ. But they will see the Father by what we call 'the beatific vision'. This is the highest part of their blessedness for here they come face to face with the infinite fountain of all blessedness. It is not a sight of the Father with the eyes, or the seeing of any form or shape, or shining light, but a seeing with one's whole soul of the unutterable glory of the Father in all his attributes. It is if you like a love of God with the whole mind, the *amor intellectualis Dei*, the perfect comprehension, admiration of the Father, and our reciprocal love of the Father as he loves us completely within the new universe, the new earth and the new city, and the new mansions, in which he has set us. This collation of all things and their relationship to the Father and the Son in their love to us is the acme of the eternal world which is ours.[1]

From this thought of progression we return specifically to the contrast between the Old Testament and the New Testament. A valid objection must be answered which can be expressed like this: Yes! I concede that there is a greater intimacy of union and communion with God Triune now than in the Old Testament, and, certainly I agree that this will be vastly increased in the next world, *but* how do you explain the intimate communion with God enjoyed by Moses, Samuel, Elijah and Daniel? And how do you explain the extraordinary intimacy of communion with God reflected in some of the psalms such as the 16th, 63rd and 86th? What about Psalm 103 which speaks of our adoption and of the great love of God for his people? My response to these questions is that it is true that some in the Old Testament were raised to the most intimate communion with God, especially those who were chosen to be instruments of revelation and authors of the infallible and holy writings. However these exceptions do not represent the generality of believers in the Old Testament. To illustrate the point some of the Judges were approved for their courage but their lives did not reflect the tenderness, compassion and

[1] John Gerstner, *Jonathan Edwards on Heaven and Hell*, Baker. Edwards develops these themes in detail under the headings 'the rationale of heaven' and 'the beatific vision', pp. 41ff.

sensitivity which flow out of our more intimate union and communion in our Triune God.

The third point of contrast with respect to the transition from the Old Testament to the New Testament is that of *abundance*. At Mount Carmel Elijah prayed fervently that the hearts of the people would be turned back. His longing was that they would repent (1 Kgs. 18:37). He was bitterly disappointed because he realised that Jezebel's hardened attitude was typical of the others. In comparison think of the tremendous ingathering of souls when the Holy Spirit was poured out at Pentecost. There was an abundance both in the numbers involved and in the diversity of people represented. There was abundance too of joy and assurance of salvation. Pentecost can be likened to the river of living water described by Ezekiel (chapter 47). It came out from under the threshold of the Temple and then seemed to miraculously increase in volume bringing life to dead areas everywhere. Fulfilled was the promise of our Lord when he lifted up his voice in the Temple and said in a loud voice, 'If a man is thirsty, let him come to me and drink. Whoever believes in me, as the Scripture has said, streams of living water will flow from within him' (John 7:37).

We pursue this matter of abundance and increase in the next chapter which is largely devoted to the subject of revival.

CHAPTER 6

BAPTISM WITH THE SPIRIT, FILLING, AND REVIVAL

Baptism is a powerful expression denoting completeness. The word is used as a metaphor to denote something overwhelming such as the flood (1 Pet. 3:10, 21), or being engulfed, as our Lord was with suffering (Matt. 20:23). It is used as an experience to denote so great a change that it translates people from one kingdom to another and into union with another (1 Cor. 10:22). As an ordinance Christian baptism likewise symbolises a union that is complete, together with a washing that is complete, that is of the whole body (Rom. 6:1-4, Heb. 10:22). Thus in keeping with its meaning we should understand that when it is said of our Lord that he will baptise with the Holy Spirit and with fire, it is meant that something overwhelming would happen.

The event signified was Pentecost. 'A sound like the blowing of a violent wind came from heaven and filled the whole house where they were sitting. They saw what seemed to be tongues of fire that separated and came to rest on each of them' (Acts 2:2,3). Thus was fulfilled our Lord's promise to baptise with the Holy Spirit and with fire.

[margin handwriting: Pentecost authenticated further the diety of Christ when the Spirit was given to the church]

The details of wind and fire are unique. One of the reasons for this event was to proclaim the fact that the Holy Spirit had been given to the Church, and that he had been given by the Lord Jesus Christ. Only God can give God. Only the Father could send Christ into the world (John 3:16). Only Christ could send the Holy Spirit into the world. Pentecost is a striking proof of the deity of Jesus.

We read that the outcome of the Holy Spirit coming in an audible and visible way was that they were all filled with him. 'All of them were filled with the Holy Spirit' (Acts 2:4). Representatives from at least fifteen widely differing nations or areas heard the Gospel in their own language.

[margin handwriting: One Baptism]

× There is an aspect in the use of the word Baptism to which reference must be made and that is its initiatory character. You are only baptised into Christ once. Christ suffered the baptism of suffering once. The Holy Spirit came from Christ exalted at the right hand of the Father for the first time at Pentecost. There can only be one first time just as there can only be one baptism.

[margin handwriting: Christ Exalted]

× For the first time the Holy Spirit came to disclose Christ's exalted glory to believers in fulfilment of John 16:14. For the first time he came in the fulness of Christ's victory and resurrection glory.

The foremost message of Pentecost was that the Holy Spirit was given to the Church. That he was Christ's gift to the whole Church to the end of time is signified by the reversal of the curse of Babel. The gift of the Holy Spirit is to every one who believes to the end of time irrespective of language or nation. He, the Holy Spirit, is Christ's gift to us, to our children, and to those furthest away from us, separated by thousands of miles or kilometres, and separated by strange languages, even to as many as the Lord our God shall call.

The restricted use of the term baptism in the New Testament

It is never said of any individual in the New Testament writings that he or she was baptised with the Holy Spirit. This restriction of the word is particularly noticeable in the case of Paul. The expression used is 'filled' (Acts 9:17). In all his writings he never ever refers to being baptised with the Spirit. If, as some hold, everything in the Christian life is contingent and dependent upon an initial fiery experience, how could Paul pass it by? It is not as though he does not tell us of his spiritual experiences. He testifies of revelations given him. These and many spiritual gifts did not come at once, as is evident from 2 Corinthians chapter 12.

[handwritten margin note: Baptism w/ th H.S. never used to describe individual experience]

Apart from Acts 1:5 and 11:16 the only other place in which the term baptism is used in Acts and the New Testament epistles in connection with the Holy Spirit is 1 Corinthians 12:13.

Both the difference and the connection between Pentecost and the baptism of 1 Corinthians 12:13 should be noted. The difference is that the latter baptism into the body of Christ refers to the regeneration of every believer together with the experimental aspect of drinking of the Spirit, whereas Pentecost refers to the body as a whole. In 1 Corinthians 12:13 the reference is to every single member of the body of Christ who has by the Spirit been made a new creature (Eph. 2:10, 2 Cor. 5:17), has had his stony heart removed and a new heart given upon which is inscribed God's laws. He is united to Christ by the Holy Spirit and at the same time incorporated into the body of the Church. All this is by agency of the Holy Spirit who has been given to him, to inhabit him wholly, work in him and transform him (Heb. 13:21, Rom. 12:2). The magnitude of this work is deserving of the term baptism of the Spirit. As I have pointed out before this is the only place where Spirit baptism is used with reference to individuals (unless we include Ephesians 4:5, Romans 6:1-5 and Galatians 3:27).

The connection between Pentecost and every individual believer referred to in 1 Corinthians 12:13 can be stated like this: Pentecost signified the gift of the Holy Spirit in the entirety of his being to the whole Church to the end of time: the baptism of each believer by the Spirit into the body ensures that person to be united in every respect with the three persons of the Trinity and with every other born again person.

The experimental aspect of Pentecost and what being filled with the Spirit means for us today

Clearly Pentecost was a spiritual experience of extraordinary proportions. As far as we know nobody from that day to this has been able to claim all the dimensions included as an experience — tongues of fire, wind, and instant coherent linguistic power. That the unique nature of the event required special emphasis has already been referred to. If we cannot expect an exact repeat, what can we expect? The description 'they were all filled with the Holy Spirit' supplies the answer. Filling with the Spirit is a responsibility which belongs to every believer. Paul exhorts all Christians to be filled with the Spirit. That exhortation comes within the context of submission to each other, marriage relationships, gratitude to God and singing praises (Eph. 5:18-20). There is no situation, challenge, or trial in this world in which the Christian cannot be filled with the Spirit. For the proclamation of the gospel to the gainsayers Peter was filled with the Spirit (Acts 4:8). All the disciples were filled with the Spirit at the prayer meeting reported in Acts 4:31. For the unpleasant task of passing judgment on an enemy of the Gospel Paul was filled with the Holy Spirit (Acts 13:9).

There is hardly a more ambitious prayer than that expressed in Ephesians 3:19, 'that you may be filled to the measure of all the fulness of God'. What is meant by this can be deduced from the context and from the parallel prayers of Ephesians 1:15-22 and Colossians 1:9-14. The Holy Spirit is called the Spirit of wisdom and revelation (Eph. 1:17), who is able to show us the full meaning of the love of Christ (Eph. 3:18,19), and give us a knowledge of God's will with spiritual wisdom and understanding (Col. 1:9). He, the Spirit of wisdom and revelation, is also able to strengthen believers with all his glorious might to exercise great endurance and patience.

There has been a tendency to confine the power of the Holy Spirit to the heroes of Gospel proclamation, but these apostolic prayers are concerned with the daily battles of life which require wisdom, endurance and patience. For all situations believers should be filled with the Holy Spirit. Even in conflicts and trials it is possible for them to be filled with the Holy Spirit and joy.

The impression is sometimes given that being filled with the Spirit is to abandon one's self-control, to lose all restraints to forsake all inhibitions, and to be swept up in an ecstasy or euphoria. To gain this objective choruses are sometimes sung repeatedly. The people are exhorted to raise their hands and give themselves over in a rising tide of emotionalism which moves towards a climax.

The Holy Spirit operates differently. He does not require an empty mind but rather fills and controls the mind. He brings order and depth to the understanding, to the affections and emotions. It was misguided to charge the disciples with being drunk early on Pentecost day. By the Spirit they were in total self-control. They demonstrated this by their discernment, initiative, courage and ability. Alcohol is destructive of the senses but the Holy Spirit is constructive. Drug taking leads to an abandonment of the intellect and a giving of the addicted to high feelings of elation which have no substance to them. Likewise in religious meetings in which emotions are whipped up there a vacuum is created. That is contrary to the mind of the Spirit.

The context of Ephesians 5:18 (Do not get drunk on wine, which leads to debauchery. Instead be filled with the Spirit.) is one which concerns holy living in the marriage, in the home, and in work. To be filled with the Spirit is to be like Joseph or Daniel in all the organisation of business affairs, and in relationships with all others. Ephesians 5:18 runs parallel with Colossians 3:16. That means that to be filled with the Holy Spirit is to be filled with thankfulness to God, to sing the praises of psalms, hymns and spiritual songs, and to be ready to submit to every order of authority created by God. None of these functions can be practically fulfilled if the mind is vacated.

The filling of the Holy Spirit leads to the heightening and enlargement of one's powers of intellect and discernment, an improvement in one's memory, efficiency in one's work performance, a warming of one's affections, an increase of zeal, and an increase all-round in the fruit of the Spirit described in Galatians 5:22.

Pentecost and revivals

Not only was Pentecost unique with regard to its fulfilment of the promise and with respect to the wind-fire phenomenon and the place and composition of the persons present, but it was unique too with regard to the power that flowed into and out of the event. Three thousand were added to the Church. The Samaritan revival reported in Acts 8, wonderful as it was, can hardly compare with Pentecost. The other instances too are hardly in the same league. I am referring now to Cornelius and his household and the Ephesus event of Acts 19.

I have shown that the New Testament never refers to an individual being baptized with fire and the Holy Spirit and that there is not so much as a hint to suggest that we are to build a doctrine of private or individual Spirit baptism experience on the foundation of Pentecost.

Revival
3

Pentecost rather was a corporate matter, and it would seem that we have here a foundation for a doctrine of revival. With regard to outpourings of the Spirit, powerful preaching and awakenings of large numbers of people, Pentecost is a prototype. We have adequately discussed the uniqueness of Pentecost day, but what about revivals in history? Surely it is correct to say that the revivals reported in the book of Acts were an extension of the powerful work of the Spirit first seen at Pentecost. There were awakenings in the Old Testament in which preaching was prominent and many people were deeply stirred. The revival at Bokim is an example (Judg. 2:1-4) and the stirring of the people by Ezra akin to it (Ezra 8:9-12). The revivals which have followed Pentecost have the same features plus the preaching of Christ crucified, risen, exalted. They have usually been preceded by intercessory prayer, often by small groups of faithful Christians. These have persevered and sometimes added fasting to their spiritual exercises. Revivals have come about through the normal ministrations of the Word. The most striking feature in revivals is the depth to which those awakened are convicted of sin, even to the point of spiritual agony. This convincing of the world of sin, righteousness and judgment by the Holy Spirit of God is the paramount need of our times.

It would be wise and beneficial if the churches today would return to the old ways of seeking revival, with the attention not so much on the quest for a sensational personal experience but rather for the outpouring of the Spirit in the awakening of the lost. I commend such books as MacFarlan's account of revivals in the 18th century, particularly at Cambuslang, and also the Authentic record of revival describing the 1859 awakening in which 39 ministers give eye witness accounts of revival. These volumes have been published by Richard Owen Roberts of Wheaton, Illinois. Mr. Roberts has also published a book describing revivals in many parts of the United States from 1815-1818. Over a hundred accounts are included. A typical description from the account of the revival at Sag-Harbour, Long Island, will give you an idea of the powerful movement of the Spirit in seasons of revival.

Sag-Harbour (Long Island). About the middle of October 1815, the Spirit was poured out from on high in plentiful effusions. Before this period, a season of awful declension prevailed. A death-like sleep seemed to have seized both saints and sinners. The church was clothed in sackcloth; she appeared forsaken and desolate. Her state was melancholy: few, very few came up to her solemn feasts; her children were discouraged; like Israel in a strange land, they seemed to have sung out their song, hung their harps on the willows, and sat down to die. The scene was truly dark and foreboding, and became more and more so every day. *O my leanness, my leanness*, was the cry of every true child of God. The wicked sat their mouths against the heavens; vice, with giant boldness, marched through the streets; Sabbath-breaking, profaneness, and intemperance, threatened to sweep away every vestige of religion: the scriptures mouldered on the shelf; the ordinances were barren, and the Spirit of prayer seemed to have taken its everlasting flight to heaven: That place was indeed *a valley of dry bones.* Rev. Mr. Gardiner the minister in that place, seemed to ascend a neighbouring hill, and survey with anguish the whitening ruins that lay below; his heart sunk at the prospect; and he exclaimed, in the language of the prophet, *Can these dry bones live?* Scarcely was the exclamation ended, when, to his utter astonishment, the breath *from the four winds* came; the slain began to stir — the dead to live. The scene was changed: the people of God began to awake; their hearts were comforted. The strong expectation that the Lord was about to appear in his glory and build up Zion, excited them to fervent supplications, to vigorous exertions.

Meetings for conference and prayer, were multiplied. Religious conversation was introduced: the attention of the whole congregation was soon aroused. The place of worship was crowded: the silence of the grave pervaded the assembly; the seriousness of eternity set on every countenance. Every ear was open, every eye was fixed; while the truth of God appeared to sink deeply into every heart. The wicked were brought to a stand; the consciences of many were awakened. Fearfulness surprised the hypocrite; sinners in Zion trembled. The anxious inquiry was made, *What shall I do to be saved?* The terrors of the law seized the hearts of many. The work of the Lord increased daily; *sinners were born of God.* The prison doors were thrown open, the chains knocked off; and numbers, delivered from the bondage of satan, were made to rejoice in the liberty of the gospel.

The work gradually progressed until about the middle of December, when the Lord seemed to rise in his might, and make bare his arm. His Spirit now like *a mighty rushing wind,* seemed to sweep all before it: the youths, the middle aged, and the man of years, fell prostrate at the foot of the cross! Often did the cry for mercy, and the song of praise, at the same moment vibrate on the ear. The footsteps of Immanuel were seen in every family, and his power felt by almost every heart. The people of God who had witnessed several revivals, filled with astonishment, would often say, that they had never beheld such a day as this before. Whenever they met there was a cordial shaking of hands and a smile of joy; while every other feeling of the soul seemed to be swallowed up in mutual love. So transporting was the scene, and so elevated were the joys of some elder Christians, that they seemed almost really to believe that the glorious morn of the latter day had commenced.

In that season of divine power, when Christ rode forth from conquering to conquer, one hundred and twenty persons, in the course of two months, expressed their hope of having passed from death unto life. These were of all ages from twelve to eighty years. This work was remarkably still and solemn. The work of conviction continued in most cases from one to three weeks, before the subjects received divine light and comfort. The veil, of sin and darkness which covered their hearts, was in many instances taken away in a moment, and the light of *the Sun of righteousness*, like a flood poured in upon the benighted mind; while in other instances, *the day spring from on high* was but just seen to glimmer, and the night of the soul to be gradually chased away as the shadows of the morning. All expressed great astonishment at their former stupidity and danger. They were overwhelmed to think that God had not cut them down, as cucumbers of the ground, and sent them to everlasting misery.

A similar book to the one from which the above extract is taken describes 25 different revivals which took place in New England during the period 1797 to 1814. We are indebted to Richard Owen Roberts for this book as well as a smaller one of 148 pages describing a revival which took place in Boston, U.S.A. in 1842. The Banner of Truth recently made available John Gillies Historical Collections of Accounts of Revival. This is a huge double column small print book of 560 pages. The title is slightly misleading since most of the volume is concerned with biography. A great deal of ground is covered in general from the 16th to the 18th centuries and many accounts of revival are included. Sprague's 'Lectures on Revivals', is a well known volume. The 162 page appendix consists of 20 letters written in 1832 by ministers who experienced revival. The book is published by The Banner of Truth.

It is very important to note that in these revivals of the past souls were added not by gathering Christians from other churches but by conversions from the unbelieving world. All evangelical churches are prospered and increased in a genuine revival and not just one brand at the expense of all the others. The revival in the city of Boston, U.S.A. from September 1841 to September 1842 provides a typical example. The increase by conversions were as follows:

14 Congregational churches increased membership from 3,902 to 5,004. (One church doubled from 105 to 210 and another increased from 56 to 182.)

9 Baptist churches increased membership from 2,817 to 4,161. (The Baptist church most affected increased from 161 to 287.)

6 Episcopal churches increased from 1,131 to 1,336.

9 Methodist Episcopal churches increased from 1,429 to 2,630.

Boston enjoyed a history of revival from the founding days of Mr. Cotton. Prior to the great Awakening in 1740 there had been a decline into Arminianism. George

Whitefield's preaching was blessed to multitudes in Boston, but even greater power was exercised through the ministry of Gilbert Tennent who watered what Whitefield had planted. One minister, a Mr. Cooper, reported that more came to him in deep concern in one week than in the whole 24 years of his preceding ministry! At the end of three months 600 had come to see him while another minister had 1,000 including boys and girls, young men and women, heads of families, aged persons, Indians and Negroes.

Just prior to the 1842 revival there was much earnest specific prayer by deeply concerned believers. The Congregational churches had struggled with a decline in doctrinal standards, having introduced error which their Puritan fathers would have regarded as subversive to the Gospel. The revival brought about a transformation not only of lives but of devotion to the truth. I have not reported the details for the increase of the Freewill Baptist churches in Boston, or for the German speaking congregations, or for the areas surrounding the city. They are recorded in detail in the book published by Mr. Roberts. All Gospel preaching churches of that city appear to have benefited from the revival.

The urgent need for revival today

We have seen that the New Testament lays great stress on conversion. Converts are taught to build their lives on the great doctrinal foundations of justification by faith, union with Christ, adoption by the Father and the indwelling ministry of the Holy Spirit. We have seen too that converts are not urged to seek a post-conversion crisis experience, and also that there is no basis for the idea that a Pentecostal experience guarantees spiritual life in a higher realm thereafter. No specifications are provided to test a crisis experience. We are not supplied with any information about the effects on the body. Tingling all over the body can be induced by different means, including music. Doubtless the variety of sensations can be brought about by other means, but we have no way of testing an individual crisis experience. That is something which is subjective. A great deal of mystique can enter into it. What we do know is that the Holy Spirit can fall upon, anoint, or fill a servant of God. The reality of that can be put to the test by observing the practical results. We can see what the Spirit-filled life is by the fruit that comes from it.

We have also seen that there are different kinds of experiences. Someone may have a heavenly experience such as the Puritan John Flavel reported, and others may experience empowerments for ministry such as D. L. Moody and R. A. Torrey testified to. In my judgment it is not helpful to read a preconceived concept of the baptism of the Spirit into these experiences even though those involved may have used that terminology. I believe the Church in this present time will be infinitely better served if we return to the emphases and terminology of our Reformed and Puritan forebears who stressed the importance of revival and sought spiritual awakening by prayer and fasting. In our local church we have a weekly prayer meeting devoted specially to intercession for revival — that is revival in ourselves personally, in our own assembly, in our nation, and to the uttermost parts of the world. At these meetings we read from revival records but always give preference to details of present day revivals such as that in Quebec Province, Canada.

In all the accounts referred to we have never come across a record of anyone predicting a forthcoming revival which would be tantamount to knowing the secret will of God (Deut. 29:29). In the Old Testament anyone making false predictions was subject to the death penalty. If only the nature of the seriousness of false prophecy was thoughtfully considered it would avert a lot of heartache and confusion. What is most impressive in all the accounts of revivals is the felt sense of the holiness of God, the awesomeness of God's justice, conviction of sin and the wonder of the way of salvation through the atoning blood of Christ — these are the main features. Many of those who experienced revival in the past believed in what they called the latter-day glory, or, Zion's bright morning. They believed that the Gospel would eventually triumph throughout the world irrespective of the enormity of the enemies set against it. They believed that Pentecost was the first New Testament revival which would be followed by outpourings of the Spirit through history, and eventually on such a scale that the Old Testament predictions of the Messiah's glorious reign will be fulfilled. I believe that there is a well grounded Biblical base for such optimism. Our ambition should always be the glory of Christ. The Holy Spirit will glorify the Son. Experiences, if genuine, will lead to God-centredness not self-centredness, and to humility rather than to inflatedness of the ego. When the Holy Spirit is given to us our experience of the love of God for us, and our love for him, are heightened (Rom. 5:5). Nobody can be made alive with Christ without experiencing a tremendous change which resounds through his whole being. The experimental outcome of the new birth occupies the whole of that person's future life. Not only does that person experience joy inexpressible, but those involved in witnessing the spiritual resurrection of that person are also deeply moved. A revival which sweeps many into God's Kingdom is like heaven on earth.

We cannot control God's Spirit. He is as sovereign as the wind (John 3:8). He will come in revivals to the end of the age, stirring the preparations for them, fulfilling them and building thereafter upon them. Whether on a large scale or a personal scale the sovereignty of the Holy Spirit must be respected. We have a responsibility to be filled with the Spirit (Eph. 5:18) which means we must not grieve him (Eph. 4:30), but rather do all things to please him. We can never control him. He is divine. There are times when we are very weak and prayerless and yet he comes mightily. At other times, even though we have been circumspect and faithful in using all the means of grace at our disposal, we still find that we are feeble. There is nothing mechanical in our relationship to the person of the Holy Spirit. We can please God and bring upon ourselves his love of complacency (John 14:21-23), but nobody, not even the Elijahs of the Church, can control the power of God. The most illustrious preachers have discovered places and come into periods when the wind was not pleased to blow. The times that the Spirit has come to blow upon the churches should always encourage us to pray.

> Oh breath of life, come sweeping through us,
> Revive thy church with life and power,
> Oh breath of life, come, cleanse, renew us,
> And fit thy church to meet this hour.

In this hour our neighbours are the starving peoples of
Africa, those oppressed by right-wing regimes in South
America, brethren persecuted by Communist regimes in
Russia and Eastern Europe. In this hour our neighbours
are engulfed by the thinking of the secular society and
dominated by principles of evolution and humanism. It is
hypocritical to pray for revival if our sincerity is not
evidenced by consistent Christian living and by genuine
evangelistic endeavour and good works. Prayer for
revival is especially the prerogative of those who have
laboured all night, who have laid their fishing nets well
and who await the result; and of those who have toiled
long in the fields and sown the seed and who now expect
the harvest. Isaiah chapter 58 is the neglected passage on
revival.

'Is not this the kind of fasting I have chosen:
   to loose the chains of injustice and untie the cords of
      the yoke,
to set the oppressed free and break every yoke? . . .
if you spend yourselves on behalf of the hungry
   and satisfy the needs of the oppressed,
then your light will rise in the darkness,
   and your night will become like the noonday.'

ACKNOWLEDGEMENTS

My indebtedness and gratitude is expressed to Pastor Al Martin for his expositions on Crisis experiences and to the Trinity Pulpit Tape Library for a series of recordings made of the Bible Class hour at Trinity Baptist Church, Montville, New Jersey, U.S.A. The series is titled 'Principles of Christian Living' (TP — M — 11 to TP — M — 19) and has the subtitle 'No crisis experience commanded'. These cassettes are highly commended. There is a slight technical difficulty inasmuch as the questions from the floor of the classroom are not always audible. These only form a small section of the material. Those questions that do come through are very helpful so turn the volume up to catch them! The first four cassettes deal with the principles involved, after which the four instances in Acts are exegeted. These tapes can be hired and details obtained from Mr. C. G. Frohwein, 15 Highfield Road, Woodford Green, Essex IG8 8JA.

BIBLIOGRAPHY

A number of books have been referred to in the footnotes
but those commended here are singled out as being
especially helpful. We have many more books available
today on Pneumatology than we do on Christology. The
following are chosen because they relate directly to the
subject of crisis experiences.

Edgar H. Andrews, *The Promise of the Spirit*, 255 pp., E.P.
1982. Douglas Judisch, *An Evaluation of Claims to the
Charismatic Gifts*, 95 pp., Baker 1978. Richard B. Gaffin,
Jr., *Perspectives on Pentecost*, 127 pp., Pres. & Ref. 1979.
A. W. Pink, *The Holy Spirit*, 192 pp., Baker. Of 32
chapters, the one on the advent of the Spirit is outstanding. Now out of print is a paperback by Kenneth Prior,
The Way of Holiness, I.V.P. A new edition has been
published in the U.S.A. It is the only book I have come
across which attempts to analyse crisis experiences. One
fairly short chapter is devoted to that theme.

What about books which extol a crisis experience for
power, holiness or assurance? These are many. So far I
have not found anything that I can recommend as a
systematic Biblical exposition. These writers differ and

disagree vastly among themselves. Some insist on tongues and some not, some hold a moderate view for sealing only, and others not, and so we could go on. Some Charismatic leaders such as Michael Green argue for the non-cessation of the extraordinary gifts, but with regard to the baptism of the Spirit hold the same approximate position as outlined in this book. cf. *I believe in the Holy Spirit*, 220 pp., Hodder 1975.

APPENDIX

THE IMPORTANCE OF PROGRESSIVE REVELATION

Fundamental to what we have considered is the question of progress in the New Testament (see preface). There are acts which are unrepeatable such as our Lord's incarnation, the giving of the Holy Spirit in a new dimension to his disciples by breathing upon them (John 20:22), and the incorporation into the church for the first time of Gentile groups (see ch. 3). We have to go further and face the question of whether apostles, prophets and the extraordinary powers with which they were endued are normative for the Church today or not. Together with the question of the baptism of the Spirit there is nothing more relevant or controversial for British evangelicalism than that question. The debate is still young. In the course of Church history other subjects have been clarified. It is not difficult to anticipate that this too will be. The purpose of this appendix or postscript is simply to refer to the importance of Biblical Theology (the study of progressive revelation), because it is this science which will settle the issue. There are materials under preparation which will be of interest to those concerned with this subject.

Of exceptional value is the work of Don Garlington,
pastor of the Baptist Church, Langley Green, Durham,
England. At the Carey Conference for ministers at
Swanwick in 1984 he read a paper on the progression of
revelation in the New Testament. The fruit of that labour
is currently appearing in *Reformation Today*. The first of
the series of articles on progressive revelation in the New
Testament appeared in *Reformation Today* 78. Basic to
our understanding of the subject is the observation that
the New Testament moves from one subject to another,
but it is equally true that unlike the Old Testament it is
one epoch in itself and not two or more epochs (the use of
the word epoch is helpful as we do not want to be
confused by the old dispensationalism which was
correct in some of its presuppositions but wrong in its
inflexible and arbitrary conclusions). The epochs of the
Old Testament are distinct from each other. The time of
Abraham is not the time of Moses and the time of Moses
is different from the epoch of Samuel. Again a distinction
can be made between the pre-exilic and the post-exilic
prophets. While distinct these periods or epochs are not
isolated from each other. One flows into the next.

These principles apply to the New Testament except
that we have one epoch. Nevertheless progress and
transition are to be observed within that epoch. For
instance there is movement from John the Baptist to the
point where Jesus takes over from John, and then again
where the apostles take over from Jesus, and yet again
when elders begin to take over from the apostles and
prophets. Within these transitions there is the major
transition of the Holy Spirit taking over from Christ (John
14:16-18).

As we move from the Gospels to the book of Acts, and then on to the letters of instruction, and finally to the Revelation we hear God saying more. We observe truth becoming more clear. This does not mean that earlier sections are less valuable or for that matter that the Old Testament is less important than the New Testament. Each Testament complements the other and each epoch with its revelatory content inter-relates and contributes to the others.

We can illustrate the principle of flow or progression by referring to church government. We do not now seek to govern the local church as Moses did (although we can learn from his meekness), and nor do we govern our churches as did Samuel (although we can learn from his example of being a systematic teacher, 1 Samuel 7:15-17). We do not govern the local church as if we were Jesus himself and certainly not as his apostles. Rather we observe the progress of revelation and see that we are led finally to the pastoral epistles where sufficient instruction is provided for us as to how the churches are to be governed to the end of the age (n.b. 1 Tim. 3 and 2 Tim. 2:2).

The principle can also be illustrated with the subject of baptism. Although it is likely that John learned the practice of immersion from the Essenes, we can say that John was the first to baptise in the New Testament epoch. He called for repentance for his baptism but spoke of Jesus who would baptise with the Holy Spirit and with fire. This Jesus did at Pentecost. Now as believers we have been incorporated into or baptised into the Trinity by the Holy Spirit. Our water baptism stanc's as the symbol of that, a portrayal which is immeasurably enriched from the events which form its background. We are helped by observing the links in the chain and by seeing what is retained and what is discarded as we move forward.

The same principles apply to the subject of prophecy which is the declaration of the mind and counsel of God. When did prophecy cease? In *Reformation Today* No. 78 Paul Noble tackles the question of Christ as prophet and whether or not he has sealed up the prophecy. The cessation of prophecy is expounded by Douglas Judisch (see bibliography). Judisch considers the relevant passages in Daniel and Zechariah. He also expounds the 1 Corinthians 13:8-13 passage well. Victor Budgen, author of the recently published biography of Hus (323 pp., E.P.) is preparing a manuscript on the subject of prophecy and tongues. He refers to many contemporary sources. Concerning the 1 Corinthians 13:8-13 passage Pastor Budgen reminds us that it is not bluster but exegesis that will decide this issue. Wayne A. Grudem is the author of *The Gift of Prophecy in 1 Corinthians*, University Press of America, Washington, D.C. This work is reviewed by Dan G. McCartney in the *Westminster Theological Journal*, Spring 1983. McCartney demonstrates the plausibility of Grudem's thesis which is to establish a halfway house for the function of prophecy. McCartney weighs the halfway house concept in the balances of Scripture and rejects it as deficient.

INDEX OF NAMES

The reader's attention is invited to follow the Contents pages for textual or contextual exposition (chapter 2 for the New Testament epistles, and chapter 3 for the book of Acts). However, in addition to some exposition under Ephesians (pp. 31ff.), the subject of sealing is developed with more definition and detail on page 92ff. Likewise the general reference to sanctification under Romans (p. 22), receives further attention on pages 63 and 80. Only a few place names are mentioned and these are easily located. An index of the names of people referred to may be useful.